THOMAS HEYWOOD

AN

APOLOGY FOR ACTORS

IN THREE BOOKS

FROM THE EDITION OF 1612, COMPARED WITH THAT OF W. CARTWRIGHT

WITH AN INTRODUCTION AND NOTES

Elibron Classics
www.elibron.com

Elibron Classics series.

© 2005 Adamant Media Corporation.

ISBN 1-4021-6180-8 (paperback)
ISBN 1-4021-3339-1 (hardcover)

This Elibron Classics Replica Edition is an unabridged facsimile of the edition published in 1841 by the Shakespeare Society, London.

Elibron and Elibron Classics are trademarks of Adamant Media Corporation. All rights reserved.

AN

APOLOGY FOR ACTORS.

IN THREE BOOKS.

BY

THOMAS HEYWOOD.

FROM THE EDITION OF 1612, COMPARED WITH THAT OF
W. CARTWRIGHT.

WITH AN INTRODUCTION AND NOTES.

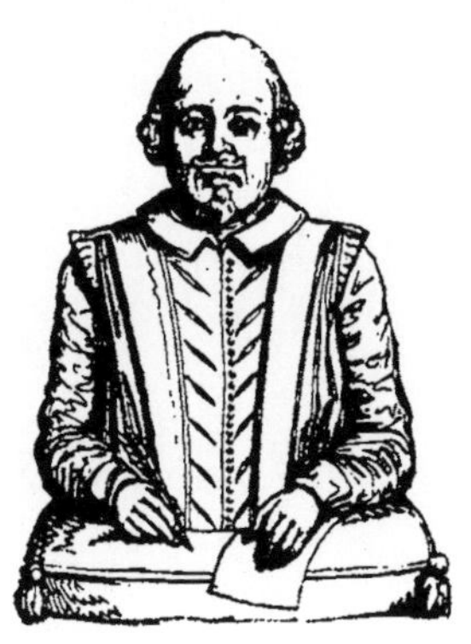

LONDON:

REPRINTED FOR THE SHAKESPEARE SOCIETY.

——

1841.

LONDON:
F. SHOBERL, JUN., 51, RUPERT STREET, HAYMARKET,
PRINTER TO H. R. H. PRINCE ALBERT.

COUNCIL

OF

THE SHAKESPEARE SOCIETY.

INTRODUCTION.

IN the cursory sketch of the various publications for and against the Stage, between the years 1578 and 1633, which precedes our reprint of Gosson's "School of Abuse," we had occasion to mention Thomas Heywood's "Apology for Actors." It is not only the most complete, but the latest regular defence of the profession, prior to the closing of the theatres on the breaking out of the Civil War. There was a pause in the literary contest subsequent to the appearance of Dr. Rainolde's "Overthrow of Stage Plays," 1599, (some copies bear the date of "Middleburgh, 1600,") and the immediate motive for the publication of Heywood's "Apology for Actors" in 1612 is not stated in the tract itself, nor elsewhere. Sir Edward Coke, indeed, in his "Charge at Norwich" in 1607, (printed by N. Butter in that year) had complained of the manner and degree in which "the country was troubled with stage-players," and denounced them from the bench ; but his reference was to actors in the provinces, who had no "commission" from the crown, nor license under the hands of any of the nobility ; and it may be asserted that for some years before Heywood's "Apology" came out, the theatres of the metropolis had been flourishing and unmolested, and had enjoyed peculiar patronage from the crown.

It was, possibly, this very state of affairs which induced Heywood to put forth his tract: the Puritans were silent, actors were prosperous, the court was favourable, and a general vindication of the profession of the Stage, as an excuse for the public and private encouragement it received, would not be unwelcome at such a juncture.

We have it on his own evidence in his "Pleasant Dialogues and Dramas," 8vo., 1637, that Heywood was a native of Lincolnshire. In the succeeding tract he notices "the time of his residence at Cambridge," and William Cartwright, (of whom we shall speak hereafter, and who reprinted "The Apology for Actors" just before the Restoration) asserts that Heywood was " a fellow of Peter House." This statement is probably correct, and nearly all his extant works display like that before us, extensive general reading, and considerable classical attainments. In what year Heywood came to London we have no account ; but on the 14th of October, 1596, a person, whose name Henslowe spells Hawode, had written " a book," or play, for the Lord Admiral's Company. On the 25th of March, 1598, we find Thomas Heywood regularly engaged by Henslowe as a player and a sharer in the company, but not as " a hireling," or mere theatrical servant receiving wages, as Malone mistakenly asserted. (Shakespeare by Boswell, III., 321). From this date, at all events, until the death of Queen Anne, the wife of James I.,

Heywood continued on the stage; for in the account of the persons who attended her funeral he is introduced as " one of her majesty's players." He wrote an ode upon her death, but he did not print it until five years afterwards as part of a much larger volume. After quitting the Lord Admiral's Company, on the accession of James I., Heywood became one of the theatrical servants of the Earl of Worcester, and was by that nobleman transferred to the queen. " I was, my lord," (says Heywood in the dedication to the Earl of Worcester of his " Nine Books of various History concerning Women," fo. 1624) "your creature, and amongst other your servants, you bestowed me upon the excellent princesse Q. Anne, * * * * but by her lamented death your gift is returned againe into your hands."

Between 1596 and 1638, he was a most voluminous playwright. When he published his "English Traveller," in 1633, he stated in a preliminary epistle, that he had written the whole, or parts of no fewer than two hundred and twenty dramatic pieces; of which, however, not more than twenty-three passed through the press. In the address " to the judicial reader," prefixed to his " Apology for Actors," 1612, he observes, " my pen hath seldome appeared in the presse till now ;" but this assertion must be taken with some qualification, and with reference, perhaps, to the many works which he had written, and which up to that year had not been printed. His earliest known work with a date is his " Edward the Fourth," a play in two parts, which was originally published in 1600. In 1605, another play

by him, called " If you know not me, you know No-
body, or the Troubles of Queen Elizabeth," was printed :
the second part of the same piece came out in 1606.
His " Fair Maid of the Exchange" and his " Woman
killed with Kindness" appeared in 1607, and his " Rape
of Lucrece" in 1608.   These were dramatic works ;
but in 1608 he put forth a translation of Salust, with
a long and laboured preface " Of the choice of
History ;" and in 1609 appeared a heroic poem in
stanzas, under the title of " Great Britains Troy." His
" Golden Age," a play, was printed the very year
before his " Apology for Actors." Thus we see that
his " pen had appeared in the press " nine times before
he wrote in 1612.

In the same spirit of allowance we must, probably,
receive another of Heywood's statements, in the course
of the work now presented to the Members of the
Shakespeare Society : — we allude to what he says on
page 16, that he is " the youngest and weakest of the
nest wherein he was hatched."   In 1612 he had been,
at least, fourteen years on the stage, and must have
been more than thirty years old. That there were
many older, as well as better actors, then living, we
need entertain no doubt ; and these he must have
had in his mind when be used the expression we have
above quoted.

No complete list has ever yet been formed of Heywood's different productions, dramatic and undramatic,
in verse and in prose.   Reed attempted it in the edition of " Dodsley's Old Plays," printed in 1780, and
made several blunders, such as attributing works by

Munday, Chettle, and Drue, to him; but much information has, of late years, been procured from sources with which Reed was not acquainted. The Shakespeare Society is preparing to print the most curious and valuable of these sources, " Henslowe's Diary," which relates to theatrical transactions in London for seventeen years subsequent to the spring of 1591. When it is published it will be seen that Heywood was engaged upon several plays, regarding which we have no other information. Until then it would be useless to attempt any exact enumeration of the varied and interesting productions of his pen. For their rarity, perhaps, we may notice his " Marriage Triumph," 1613, on the union between the Prince Palatine and the Princess Elizabeth; and his " Elegy on the Death of James I., 1625. In the last he informs us that, at one time (the date is not given) he had been the theatrical servant of the Earl of Southampton, the patron of Shakespeare. Heywood also wrote all the known pageants for Lord Mayor's Day, between 1630 and 1640, when they ceased for some years to be exhibited.

We know nothing of the later incidents of his life beyond those furnished by the publication of his many works, the last, perhaps, being " The Life of Ambrosius Merlin," which came out in 1641. In that year he is mentioned in some verses inserted in " Wit's Recreations," having reference principally to his " Hierarchy of the Blessed Angels," which had appeared in 1635. When he published that collection of his minor pieces, called " Pleasant Dialogues and Dramas," in 1637, he was evidently in considerable pecuniary distress, and he seems to have sustained a long contest with poverty, not terminated until his decease. In 1648, in the "Satire against Separatists," he is spoken of as if he were still alive; and this seems to be the last trace of him. If he died in that year, he just outlived the issue of the notorious "Ordnance of the Lords and Commons assembled in Parliament," for the entire suppression of theatrical amusements.

William Cartwright's republication of Heywood's "Apology for Actors," shortly prior to the Restoration, has been already noticed. That republication has no date; but the late Mr. Douce, whose evidence on such a point is generally to be taken as conclusive, in his "Illustrations of Shakespeare," I., p. 300, tells us that it was printed in 1658. Cartwright was at this period a bookseller; but he did not intend that Heywood's tract should appear to be a mere reprint: he therefore altered the title of it, and called it "The Actor's Vindication;" and in the dedication to the Marquess of Dorchester, he states that the author had written it "not long before his death." The object was to give the work a more modern air, and greater weight of authority, than it would have possessed had Cartwright stated that it originally came out forty-six years before he revived it. For the same reason he modernized the style in several respects, gave only the initials of the "friends and fellows" of Heywood, who in 1612 had signed their laudatory lines at length, and inserted a passage in praise of Edward Alleyn, and speaking of him as dead, which Heywood could not have written in 1612, because the subject of the eulogium did not die until fourteen years afterwards.

" Among so many dead," says Heywood, " let me not forget one yet alive, in his time the most worthy, famous Maister Edward Alleyn ;" to which, in 1658, Cartwright, omitting " one yet alive," added as follows : — " who, in his lifetime, erected a College at Dulwich for poor people, and for education of youth. When this College was finished, this famous man was so equally mingled with humility and charity, that he became his own pensioner, humbly submitting himself to that proportion of diet and clothes which he had bestowed on others, and afterwards was interred in the same College." The expression by Heywood, in 1612, that Alleyn, " in his time," was " the most worthy," shews that he certainly had retired from the stage before that year.

An actor, of the name of William Cartwright, belonged, in 1613, to an Association of Players with which Henslowe was connected ; and, as has been shown in the " Memoirs of Edward Alleyn," p. 153, he was often one of the guests of the Founder of Dulwich College between the years 1617 and 1622. He was in all likelihood the father of the William Cartwright who, just before dramatic performances were recommenced, but while the theatres were still closed, was a bookseller, but who had no doubt been an actor prior to the breaking out of the Civil War, and certainly was so for many years after the Restoration. Downes frequently introduces his name in his *Roscius Anglicanus*, 1708, as one of the King's Company, as-

sembled immediately on the return of Charles II. He
was Corbachio in " Volpone," Morose in " Epicœne,"
Mammon in " the Alchemist," Brabantio in " Othello,"
and Falstaff in the first part of " Henry the Fourth,"
besides filling many other parts in modern plays. He
continued on the stage after the union of the King's
and the Duke's Companies in 1682, and died in 1687,
leaving his books, pictures, &c., to Dulwich College,
where his father had been so often hospitably received,
and of the benefits of which institution he must himself have been a witness.

At the time of his death two persons, named Francis
and Jane Johnson, husband and wife, lived with Cartwright as servants, and had done so for about seventeen
years. They seem to have taken possession of all his
personal property, including plate, pictures, books, and
490 broad pieces of gold. Proceedings in Chancery
were accordingly instituted against them by the Master,
Warden, Fellows, &c., of Dulwich College, about the
year 1689, and Francis Johnson was thrown into prison,
where he remained for two years. These facts, and
some others of a singular nature, and quite new in the
life of Cartwright, are contained in what forms the
commencement of the answer of Francis and Jane
Johnson to the bill filed by the College, preserved
among the archives at Dulwich. The conclusion of the
document is unfortunately lost, but that portion which
remains seems to contain nearly all the particulars of
the case, and we subjoin it as a curious relic relating to
the biography of a very eminent performer, one of the.

last disciples in what may be termed the School of Shakespeare.

> " The joint and several Answers of Francis Johnson and Jane
> his wife, Defendants to the Bill of Complaint of the Master,
> Warden, Fellows, six poor Brethren and six poor Sisters
> and twelve poor Scholars of Dulwich College, otherwise
> called the College of God's Gift, within the parish of Cam-
> berwell in the county of Surry, Complainants.

" The said Defts and either of them, saving and reserving to each other all due benefit and advantage of exceptions to the incertainties and insufficiencies of the Complainants bill of complaint, for answer thereto, or so much thereof as concerns them or either of them to make answer unto, they answer and say as followeth—And first this Deft Francis Johnson for his part saith that he cannot more fully or particularly make answer to any the matters or charges of the Comp^ts bill laid to his charge, then within and by his former answer by him put in thereto is already set forth and expressed ; for he saith that he did not intermeddle with any part of the personal estate of William Cartwright deceased, in the bill named, otherwise then is hereinafter set forth in his this Defts wife's answer, she being the only person generally entrusted by the said Mr. Cartwright to look after and take care of his concernes at home. And this Deft was employed as his servant to look after his affairs in their Maties play-house and to receive his, the said Mr Cartwright's, allowance out of the profits of the said playhouse, he being one of the Players there, and to pay the same unto him, which he accordingly did for about the space of 17 years that he lived with him as his servant, and was by agreement to have had from his said Master an allowance of £15 per Annum during the time he lived with him ; but saith there was about 5 years arrears of the said allowance due to this Deft at the time of the decease of the said William Cartwright. And the said Jane Johnson for her part saith, that the said William Cartwright departed this life about the middle of December, 1687, being then possessed of divers goods, household stuff and other personal estate, which he had in the house wherein he died situate in or near Lincolns Inn Fields in the County of Middx hereinafter mentioned. And farther saith that in or about the month of January then next, that the Sheriffs officers of the said County, by virtue of some authority, as they alleged, and by the directions of the Comp[ts.] as this Deft hath been credibly informed [did] seize and take away, not only most of the goods in the said house (save what is hereinafter mentioned) and carried them away and never returned the same, but also took and carried away divers goods and apparels of these Defts which are hereafter named, vizt. some new linen cloth, some part thereof being cut out for divers uses, both which, as well the cut as otherwise, they took away, being of the value of £5 and upwards, as also divers wearing apparel of her, this Deft and her said husband, worth about £10; and did also take away two beds, a fine fleeced wool blanket and two large chests, together with a trunk and box both full of linen, as likewise a jack, fire irons, andyrons, tongs and fireshovel, as also a rosting iron, several joint stools, a large Indian bason and jug, with divers other things, and the which goods were never appraised by the said officers nor ever returned again to these Defts, nor to any other person or persons for their use, or any recompence or satisfaction for the same. And as to the goods of M[r] Cartwright which came to this Defts possession, and were by her disposed of, and which are all the goods of him and that he died possessed of that ever came to the custody of this Deft or her said husband to her knowledge or belief, or into the hands custody or power of any other person or persons for their or either of their use or uses, which are as followeth, viz two silver tankards, gilt, which she pawned for £4 a piece, and which were disposed of by the Pawnbroker, in regard the money lent thereupon, and the interest demanded, did amount, as the Pawnbroker pretended, to the intrinsic value of the said plate : one small amber box or cabinet which this Deft did pawn for 40s. and believes it is not worth much more : six books of prints which she sold for £3 : six volumes of play books, which she sold for 20s. : several small pictures which she sold for 15s. : a Turkey carpet which she sold for about 13 or 14s. : a pair of old decayed brass candlesticks and brass fire irons sold at 6s. 8d. And this Deft doth verily believe in her conscience, and is well assured that there was no other or further benefit made of the said goods in any manner of way whatsoever than before mentioned. And this Deft confesseth that there came to her hands and custody 490 broad pieces of the gold of the said Mr Cartwright, out of which this Deft paid for the burying of the said Mr Cartwright about the sum of £33 : paid for rent arrear owing by him £5 10s. 0 : paid Mr Austin the victualler for a score of beer and ale £4 12s. 0d. : paid to his milkwoman £1 19s. 3d. : paid for his score at the Tavern £1 2s. 0d. or thereabouts : paid his washerwoman a guinea. And further this Deft saith that she and her said husband did constantly live with the said Mr Cartwright as his servants for the space of 17 years and upwards, during all which time he did agree to allow unto this Defts said husband at the rate of £15 per ann. as is hereinbefore specified. And this Deft doth verily believe that there was 4 or 5 years arrears of wages due to her said husband at the time of the death of their said Master; and like-wise saith that the said Mr Cartwright did agree to give and allow unto her this Deft the sum of £10 per ann. for 12 of the 17 years, and to allow her £13 pounds for the last 5 years, in regard this Deft during the said 5 years undertook all the work of the house without an under servant, which before that time had been kept; but yet this Deft could never receive any money from him or other satisfaction for her said wages during all his life time; and saith that her whole wages for the said 17 years was wholly unsatisfied to her at the time of Mr Cartwright's death, and [he] did from time to time excuse the payment thereof, pretending that he would when he died leave all his estate to this Deft and her said husband, withall declaring that he kept nothing from this Deft, and that she had all or most of his estate in her hands and power, and what would she desire more of him, or words to that or the like purpose : and he by such insinuations and promises did from time to time keep off this Deft from receiving any part of her wages, notwithstanding she was a continual slave to him and seldom suffered to go abroad, for that when he was at home he required the Deft to give him diligent and constant attendance there, being aged and often infirm, and when he was abroad he would not trust any person in his house besides this Deft, by reason of which confinement this Deft could not have time for near 17 years together to go to Church to serve God. By all which it is very manifest that this Deft had a very uncomfortable living during all her service with her said Master, whenas when she was prevailed with to come and

live with him as his housekeeper, she was in a good way of living,
using the trade of a button maker, by which she did make considerable profit.   And this Deft moreover saith that her said Master, towards part of satisfaction of the kindness intended her, this Deft,
and her said husband for all the service and slavery aforesaid,
did some time in his life time execute some deed in writing, whereby he did (as these Defts are advised) settle the sum of £16
per ann., chargeable by way of annuity or rent charge out of some
houses in or about the city of London, to be payable to this Deft
and her said husband during their lives and the life of the longer
liver of them; and they did accordingly receive the said rent for
some small time after the death of her said Master, and until about
Midsummer 1689, at or about which time the Compl[ts] did (as this
Deft is informed) obtain some order of this honourable Court whereby
to restrain this Deft and her said husband from further receiving the
said rent of £16 per Ann: but for what reason, and whether the said
order be still in force or not, this Deft knoweth not.   And matters
thus standing, and there having been very hot prosecutions in this
honourable Court and elsewhere against her and her said husband by
the Compl[ts], and they having caused him to be imprisoned did remaine a prisoner for about the space of two years.   And this Deft
saith that a great number of the said broad pieces were expended in
paying the debts aforesaid of her said Master, and in defending of
the suite aforesaid, as also in maintaining her husband in prison
during the time aforesaid and procuring his enlargement, and likewise in maintaining these Defts with meat and drink and other necessaries ever since the payment of the said annuity hath been kept
from them, being about 4 years and an half since.   And this Deft
further likewise saith that some yeares since, she finding that all the
said broad pieces (except 140) were by the means aforesaid spent and
consumed, she did deposite the same in the hands of one M[r] Nicholas
Archibold, her counsell, desiring that he would treat with the said
Compl[ts], and endeavour to persuade them (having consideration to
these Defts payments, troubles and expenses aforesaid) to accept of
the said 140 pieces in full satisfaction for all such part of the several
estate of her said Master as came into these Defts hands, or used
words to that purpose, and her said Counsell did upon reception of

the said pieces promise so to do, but having once got possession thereof, he did still put this Deft off with some pretence or other, and so still neglected to proceed therein and did "—[*cætera desunt*].

The precise result of this suit in Chancery does not appear from any document we have been able to consult, but it is certain that Dulwich College obtained most of the books and pictures which had belonged to Cartwright: the latter have, we believe, been preserved, the most valuable being the portraits of Burbage, Field, Bond, Cartwright, and some others of the same class; but the books, consisting mainly of old plays (such probably as the six volumes mentioned in the preceding Answer, which Mrs. Johnson sold for 20*s*.) have almost entirely disappeared. The late Mr. Malone was lucky enough to induce the Master, Warden, and Fellows to exchange the old Plays for old Sermons, and the old Plays now form the bulk of the Commentator's collection at Oxford. One of the books left by Cartwright to the College, and still preserved in the library, is a copy of his republication of Heywood's " Apology for Actors."

Among other remarkable points adverted to in that work is one which has of late attracted considerable attention, in consequence chiefly of a very interesting and ingenious letter from Mr. W. J. Thoms to Mr. Amyot, the Treasurer of the Society of Antiquaries, published in the New Monthly Magazine for January, 1841. Professor Tieck, of Dresden, first started the notion that a company of English Players, having found their way into Germany, performed English plays in different towns, which never were printed excepting in

German versions. Heywood's " Apology for Actors" puts the matter beyond doubt, that several companies of performers from this country were retained on the continent, under royal and noble patronage, late in the sixteenth, and early in the seventeenth centuries. It is not necessary here to enter into particulars, because they will be found inserted hereafter. We only allude to them as a singular confirmation of a modern theory; and Mr. Thoms has undertaken to furnish the Shakespeare Society with translations of four German Dramas, taken, as he supposes, from old English plays not now known to exist, but which Shakespeare employed more or less in the composition of some of his works.

We have evidence that Heywood was for many years engaged upon a collection of the Lives of Poets of his own day and country, as well as of other times and nations. It would of course have included Shakespeare, and his dramatic predecessors and contemporaries; and it is possible that the MS., or part of it, may yet lurk in some unexplored receptacle. Richard Brathwayte, in his " Scholars' Medley," 1614, gave the earliest information of Heywood's intention to make " a description of all Poets' lives;" and, ten years afterwards, in his " Nine Books of various History concerning Women," Heywood himself tells us that the title of his projected work would be " The Lives of all the Poets, modern and foreign." It was still in progress in 1635, when " the Hierarchy of the Blessed Angels" came out, on p. 245 of which work we meet with the following passage :—" In proceeding farther I might have forestalled a work, which hereafter (I hope) by God's assistance to commit to the public view; namely, the Lives of all the Poets, foreign and modern, from the first before Homer, to the *novissimi* and last, of what nation or language soever."

The manner in which he would probably have treated the subject makes us still more regret the loss of his collection of the Lives of the Poets; and we may judge of that manner from the terms in which he speaks of his great contemporaries in the body of the work just quoted, p. 206. What he says of them affords a curious proof of the kindly and familiar footing on which they lived with each other, and, as the passage is little known, we shall venture to quote the whole of it.

" Greene, who had in both Academies ta'ne
Degree of Master, yet could never gaine
To be call'd more than *Robin*; who, had he
Profest aught save the Muse, serv'd and been free
After a seven-yeares' prenticeship, might have
(With credit too) gone Robert to his grave.
Marlo, renowned for his rare art and wit,
Could ne're attaine beyond the name of *Kit*,
Although his Hero and Leander did
Merit addition rather. Famous Kid
Was called but *Tom*. *Tom* Watson, though he wrote
Able to make Apollo's selfe to dote
Upon his Muse, for all that he could strive,
Yet never could to his full name arrive.
Tom Nash (in his time of no small esteeme)
Could not a second syllable redeeme.
Excellent Bewmont, in the foremost ranke
Of the rar'st wits, was never more than *Franck*.
Mellifluous Shakespeare, whose inchanting quill
Commanded mirth or passion, was but *Will*;

> And famous Johnson, though his learned pen
> Be dipt in Castaly, is still but *Ben*.
> Fletcher add Webster, of that learned packe
> None of the mean'st, yet neither was but *Jacke*.
> Dekker's but *Tom ;* nor May nor Middleton ;
> And hee's now but *Jacke* Foord that once was John."

We can figure to ourselves no higher prize, of a literary kind, than the discovery of the MS. of the lives of such men by such a man, who would probably have given us their great characteristics and individual peculiarities, and have dwelt with fond detail upon the scenes of their early and social intercourse. Let us hope that the labours and researches of the Shakespeare Society, and of those who are anxious to promote its objects, may hereafter bring some such materials to light.

AN

APOLOGY

FOR ACTORS.

Containing three briefe

Treatises.

1. *Their Antiquity.*
2. *Their ancient Dignity.*
3. *The true use of their Quality.*

Written by Thomas Heywood.

Et prodesse solent et delectare——

LONDON:

Printed by *Nicholas Okes.*

1612.

To the Right Honourable Edward, Earle of
Worcester, Lord of Chepstoll, Ragland, and
Gower, Knight of the most Noble Order
of the Garter, Maister of the Horse,
and one of the King's most
Honourable Privy
Councel.

KNOWING all the vertues and endowments of nobility,
which florisht in their height of eminence in your Ancestors,
now, as by a divine legacy and lineall inheritance, to survive
in you, and so consequently from you to your truly ennobled
issue (Right Honourable), I presumed to publish this unworthy worke under your gracious patronage. First, as an ac-
knowledgement of that duty I am bound to you in as a
servant: next, assured that your most judiciall censure is as
able to approve what therein is authentike and good, as your
noble and accustomed modesty will charitably connive, if
there be any thing therein unworthy your learned approbation. I have striv'd (my Lord) to make good a subject, which
many through envy, but most through ignorance, have sought
violently (and beyond merit) to oppugne; in which, if they
have either wandred through spleene, or erred by non-know-
ledge, I have (to my power) plainly and freely illustrated;
propounding a true, direct, and faithfull discourse, touching
the antiquity, the ancient dignity, and the true use of Actors,
and their quality. If my industry herein be by the common
adversary harshly received, but by your Honour charitably
censured, I have from the injuditious (whom I esteeme not)
but what I expect, but from your Lordship (whom I ever
reverence) more then I can merit.

Your Honour's humbly devoted,

THOMAS HEYWOOD.

B 2

To my good Friends and Fellowes
the Citty-Actors.

OUT of my busiest houres I have spared my selfe so much time, as to touch some particulars concerning us, to approve our antiquity, ancient dignity, and the true use of our quality. That it hath beene ancient, we have derived it from more then two thousand yeeres agoe successively to this age. That it hath beene esteemed by the best and greatest, to omit all the noble patrons of the former world, I need alledge no more then the royall and princely services in which we now live. That the use thereof is authentique, I have done my endeavour to instance by history, and approve by authority. To excuse my ignorance in affecting no florish of eloquence to set a glosse upon my Treatise, I have nothing to say for my selfe but this :— a good face needs no painting, and a good cause no abetting. Some over-curious have too liberally taxed us; and hee (in my thoughts) is held worthy reproofe, whose ignorance cannot answere for it selfe : I hold it more honest for the guiltlesse to excuse, then the envious to exclaime; and we may as freely (out of our plainnesse) answere, as they (out of their perverseness) object, instancing my selfe by famous Scaliger, learned Doctor Gager, Doctor Gentiles, and others, whose opinions and approved arguments on our part I have in my briefe discourse altogether omitted, because I am loath to bee taxed in borrowing from others; and besides, their workes, being extant to the world, offer themselves freely to every man's perusall. I am profest adversary to none : I rather covet reconcilement then opposition, nor proceedes this my labour from any envy in me, but rather to shew them wherein they erre. So, wishing you judiciall audiences, honest poets, and true gatherers, I commit you all to the fulnesse of your best wishes.

Your's ever,

T. H.

TO THE JUDICIALL
READER.

I HAVE undertooke a subject (curteous reader) not of suffi-cient countenance to bolster it selfe by his owne strength, and therefore have charitably reached it my hand to support it against any succeeding adversary. I could willingly have committed this worke to some more able then my selfe, for the weaker the combatant, hee needeth the stronger armes; but in extremities I hold it better to weare rusty armour then to gœ naked: yet if these weake habiliments of warre can but buckler it from part of the rude buffets of our adversaries, I shall hold my paines sufficiently guerdoned. My pen hath seldome appeared in presse till now: I have beene ever too jealous of mine owne weaknesse willingly to thrust into the presse; nor had I at this time, but that a kind of necessity enjoyned me to so sudden a businesse. I will neither shew my selfe over presumtuous in skorning thy favour, nor too im-portunate a beggar by too servilly intreating it. What thou art content to bestow upon my pains, I am content to accept: if good thoughts, they are all I desire: if good words, they are more then I deserve: if bad opinion, I am sorry I have incur'd it: if evil language, I know not how I have merited it: if any thing, I am pleased: if nothing, I am satisfied, con-tenting my selfe with this—I have done no more then (had I beene called to account) shewed what I could say in the de-fence of my owne quality.

Thine,

T. HEYWOOD.

Firma valent per se, nullumque Machaona quærunt.

Ἀπολογία τῶν πανηγυρῶν.

Τοῦτο βροτοῖσι μελεῖ μουσῶν περικαλλέα ὑμνεῖν
Καὶ κλέα καὶ δ' ἀρετῆς ; ἔραμαι μέγα ; τὸν γὰρ ἀλιτρὸν
Εὗρε Θεός ; φιλικὸν μέλος ἀνθρώποισι πονηρὸν
Φεῦγε, μιθεὶς τῶν κῶμα κακῶν· κωμῳδία δέξει
Τὴν δὲ ὑποθήκην ; μήτε καλ' ἔργα τραγῳδία κάρφει·
Ἀγριός εἷ ; καὶ ὁρᾷς, ὅτι φαῦλος ὅμως θ' ὑπερόπτης
Βάλλετο, καὶ παραπόλλετο δ' ἐν μεγάλοισι θεάτροις·
Ἀλλ' ἀγαθῶν αἰεὶ δυνάμεις καλεαὶ φερέονται.
Εἰ φιλέῃς μούσας, φιλέειν δεῖ εὐρὰ θέατρα,
Αἰσχρὰ διώκων· καιρὸν καὶ φίλον ἄνδρ' ἀπολέσσῃς,

Αλ. Πρ'.

In laudem, nec Operis, nec Authoris.

Fallor ? an hæc solis non solùm grata Theatris ?
(Esse putes solis quanquam dictata Theatris)
Magna sed a sacro veniet tibi gratia Templo,
Parve Liber ; proles haut infitianda parenti.
Plurimus hunc nactus librum de-plebe-Sacerdos
(Copia verborum cui sit, non copia rerum)
Materiæ tantum petet hinc ; quantum nec in uno
Promere mense potest, nec in uno forsitan anno.
Da quemuis textum ; balbâ de nare locutus,
Protinùs exclamat (nefanda piacula !) in urbe
(Proh dolor !) impietas nudatâ fronte vagatur !
Ecce librum (Fratres) damnando authore poëtâ :
Pejorem nec sol vidit, nec Vorstius ipse
Hæresiarcha valet componere : Quippe Theatri
Mentitas loquitur laudes (ó tempora), laudet
Idem si potis est, monachum, monachine cucullum.
Sacro quis laudes unquam nomenve Theatri
Repperit in CANONE? *haud vllus. stolidissime, dogma*
Non CANONEM *sapit hoc igitur, sed Apocryphon. Inde*
(Lymphatum attonito pectus tundente popello,
Et vacuum quassante caput mæstumque tuenti)
Sic multo raucùm crocitans sudore perorat ;

Quod non dant proceres dedit histrio : nempe benignam
Materiam declamandi, plebemque docendi.
Quis tamen hic mystes tragico qui fulmina ab ore
Torquet? Num doctus? Certé. Num metra Catonis
Quatuor edidicit, tolidem quoque commata Tullí.
Jejunamque catechesin pistoribus æquè
Sartoribusque piis scripsit.   Liber utilis his, qui
Baptistam simulant vultu, Floralia vivunt :
Queisque supercilio brevior coma.   Sed venerandos
Graios hic Latiosque patres exosus ad unum est ;
Et Canones damnans fit Apocryphus.   Uritur intùs.
Laudibus ACTORIS *multùm mordetur. Ab illo*
Laude suâ fraudatur enim.   Quis nescit?   Ini-
      quum'st
Præter se scripto laudetur (a) *Hypocrita quisquam.*
Fallor? an hæc solis non solùm grata Theatris?

(a)Hypocrita propriè personatum histrionem denotat.

     Anonymus, sive.
     pessimus omnium Poëta.

To them that are opposite to this worke.

Cease your detracting tongues, contest no more,
Leave off for shame to wound the Actor's fame,
Seeke rather their wronged credit to restore ;
Your envy and detractions quite disclaime.
    You that have termed their sports lascivious, vile,
    Wishing good princes would them all exile,
    See here this question to the full disputed ;
    Heywood hath you, and all your proofes confuted.

Wouldst see an emperour and his counsell grave,
  A noble souldier acted to the life,
  A Romane tyrant, how he doth behave
  Himselfe at home, abroad, in peace, in strife?

Wouldst see what's love, what's hate, what's foule excesse,
Or wouldst a traytor in his kind expresse ?
Our Stagerites can (by the poet's pen)
Appeare to you to bee the selfe same men.

What though a sort for spight, or want of wit,
Hate what the best allow, the most forbeare,
What exercise can you desire more fit
Than stately stratagemes to see and heare ?
    What profit many may attaine by playes,
    To the most critticke eye this booke displaies   Vid. Page 5.
    Brave men, brave acts, being bravely acted too,
    Makes, as men see things done, desire to do.

And did it nothing, but in pleasing sort
Keepe gallants from mispending of their time,
It might suffice ; yet here is nobler sport,
Acts well contriv'd, good prose, and stately rime.
    To call to church Campanus bels did make ;
    Playes dice and drinke invite men to forsake :
    Their use being good, then use the Actors well,
    Since our's all other nation's farre excell.

AR. HOPTON.

To his beloved friend, Maister

THOMAS HEYWOD.

Sume superbiam quæsitam meritis.

I cannot, though you write in your owne cause,
    Say you deale partially ; but must confesse,
(What most men wil) you merit due applause,
    So worthily your worke becomes the presse.

And well our Actors may approve your paines,
  For you give them authority to play,
Even whilst the hottest plague of envy raignes ;
  Nor for this warrant shall they dearly pay.

What a full state of poets have you cited
  To judge your cause ; and to our equal view
Faire monumentall theaters recited,
  Whose ruines had bene ruin'd but for you !

Such men, who can in tune both raile and sing,
  Shall, viewing this, either confesse 'tis good,
Or let their ignorance condemn the spring,
  Because 'tis merry, and renewes our bloud.

Be, therefore, your owne iudgement your defence,
  Which shall approve you better then my praise,
Whilst I, in right of sacred innocence,
  Durst ore each guilded tombe this knowne truth raise :
Who dead would not be acted by their will,
It seemes such men have acted their lives ill.

        By your friend,

            JOHN WEBSTER.

To my loving friend and fellow,

THOMAS HEYWOOD.

Thou that do'st raile at me for seeing a play,
How wouldst thou have me spend my idle houres ?
Wouldst have me in a taverne drinke all day,
Melt in the sunne's heate, or walke out in showers ?

Gape at the Lottery from morne till even,
To heare whose mottoes blankes have, and who prises?
To hazzard all at dice (chance six or seven)
To card or bowle? my humour this dispises.

But thou wilt answer: None of these I need,
Yet my tir'd spirits must have recreation.
What shall I doe that may retirement breed,
Or how refresh my selfe, and in what fashion?

To drabbe, to game, to drinke, all these I hate:
Many enormous things depend on these.
My faculties truely to recreate
With modest mirth, and my selfe best to please,

Give me a play, that no distaste can breed.
Prove thou a spider, and from flowers sucke gall;
I'le, like a bee, take hony from a weed;
For I was never puritannicall.

I love no publicke soothers, private scorners,
That raile 'gainst letchery, yet love a harlot:
When I drinke, 'tis in sight, and not in corners;
I am no open saint, and secret varlet.

Still, when I come to playes, I love to sit
That all may see me in a publike place,
Even in the stages front, and not to git
Into a nooke, and hood-winke there my face.

*This is the difference: such would have men deeme
Them what they are not; I am what I seeme.*

RICH. PERKINS.

———

To my good friend and fellow,
THOMAS HEYWOOD.

Let others taske things honest, and to please
Some that pretend more strictnesse then the rest,
Exclaime on playes, know I am none of these
That in-ly love what out-ly I detest.
Of all the modern pastimes I can finde
To content me, of playes I make best use,
As most agreeing with a generous minde :
There see I vertues crowne, and sinnes abuse.
   Two houres well spent, and all their pastimes done,
   What's good I follow, and what's bad I shun.

CHRISTOPHER BEESTON.

To my good friend and fellow,
THOMAS HEYWOOD.

Have I not knowne a man, that to be hyr'd
Would not for any treasure see a play,
Reele from a taverne?   Shall this be admir'd,
When as another, but the t'other day,
   That held to weare a surplesse most unmeet,
   Yet after stood at Paul's-crosse in a sheet.

ROBERT PALLANT.

To my approved good friend
M. THOMAS HEYWOOD.

Of thee, and thy Apology for playes,
I will not much speake in contempt or praise;
Yet in these following lines I'le shew my minde
Of playes, and such as have 'gainst playes repin'd.

A play's a briefe epitome of time,
Where man my see his vertue or his crime
Lay'd open, either to their vice's shame,
Or to their vertues' memorable fame.
A play's a true transparant christall mirror,
To shew good minds their-mirth, the bad their terror :
Where stabbing, drabbing, dicing, drinking, swearing,
Are all proclaim'd unto the sight and hearing,
In ugly shapes of heaven-abhorrid sinne,
Where men may see the mire they wallow in.
And well I know it makes the divell rage,
To see his servants flouted on a stage.
A whore, a thiefe, a pander, or a bawd,
A broker, or a slave that lives by fraud ;
An usurer, whose soule is in his chest,
Until in hell it comes to restlesse rest ;
A fly-blowne gull, that faine would be a gallant ;
A raggamuffin that hath spent his tallant ;
A self-wise foole, that sees his wits out-stript,
Or any vice that feeles it selfe but nipt,
Either in Tragedy or Comedy,
In Morall, Pastorall, or History,
But straight the poyson of their envious tongues,
Breakes out in vollyes of calumnious wronges,
And then a tinker, or a dray-man sweares,
I would the house were fir'd about their eares.
Thus when a play nips Sathan by the nose,
Streight all his vassals are the actor's foes.
But feare not, man, let envy swell and burst,
Proceed, and let the divell do his worst ;
For playes are good, or bad, as they are us'd,
And best inventions often are abused.

Your's ever,
JOHN TAYLOR.

The Author to his Booke.

The world's a theater, the earth a stage,
Which God and nature doth with actors fill :
Kings have their entrance in due equipage,
And some there parts play well, and others ill.
The best no better are (in this theater),
Where every humor's fitted in his kinde ;
This a true subiect acts, and that a traytor,
The first applauded, and the last confin'd ;
This plaies an honest man, and that a knave,
A gentle person this, and he a clowne,
One man is ragged, and another brave :
All men have parts, and each man acts his owne.
She a chaste lady acteth all her life ;
A wanton curtezan another playes ;
This covets marriage love, that nuptial strife ;
Both in continual action spend their dayes :
Some citizens, some soldiers, borne to adventer,
Sheepheards, and sea-men. Then our play's begun
When we are borne, and to the world first enter,
And all finde exits when their parts are done.
If then the world a theater present,
As by the roundnesse it appears most fit,
Built with starre galleries of hye ascent,
In which Jehove doth as spectator sit,
And chiefe determiner to applaud the best,
And their indevours crowne with more then merit ;
But by their evill actions doomes the rest
To end disgrac't, whilst others praise inherit ;
He that denyes then theaters should be,
He may as well deny a world to me.

THOMAS HEYWOOD.

AN APOLOGY FOR

Actors ; and first touching

their Antiquity.

Mooved by the sundry exclamations of many seditious sectists in this age, who, in the fatnes and ranknes of a peacable common-wealth, grow up like unsavery tufts of grasse, which, though outwardly greene and fresh to the eye, yet are they both unpleasant and unprofitable, beeing too sower for food, and too ranke for fodder; these men, like the ancient Germans, affecting no fashion but their owne, would draw other nations to bee slovens like them-selves, and, under-taking to purifie and reforme the sacred bodies of the church and common-weale (in the trew use of both which they are altogether ignorant), would but like artlesse phisitions, for ex-periment sake, rather minister pils to poyson the whole body, then cordials to preserve any, or the least part. Amongst many other thinges tollerated in this peaceable and florishing state, it hath pleased the high and mighty princes of this land to limit the use of certain publicke theaters, which, since many of these over-curious heads have lavishly and violently slan-dered, I hold it not amisse to lay open some few antiquities to approve the true use of them, with arguments (not of the least moment) which, according to the weaknes of my spirit and infancy of my iudgment, I will (by God's grace) commit to the eyes of all favorable and iudiciall readers, as well to satisfie the requests of some of our well qualified favorers, as to stop the envious acclamations of those who chalenge to themselves a priveledge[d] invective, and against all free estates a railing liberty. Loath am I (I protest), being the youngest and weakest of the nest wherin I was hatcht, to soare this pitch before others of the same brood, more fledge, and of better winge then my selfe; but though they whome more especially this taske concernes, both for their ability in writing and sufficiency in judgement (as their workes generally witnesse to the world) are content to over-slip so necessary a subject, and have left it as to mee, the most unworthy, I thought it better to stammer out my mind, then not to speake at all; to scrible downe a marke in the stead of writing a name, and to stumble on the way, rather then to stand still and not to proceede on so necessary a journey.

Nox erat, et somnus lassos submisit ocellos. It was about that time of the night when darknes had already overspread the world, and a husht and generall sylence possest the face of the earth, and men's bodyes, tyred with the businesse of the daye, betaking themselves to their best repose, their never-sleeping soules labored in uncoth dreames and visions, when suddenly appeared to me the tragicke Muse, *Melpomene,*

> ———— *animosa Tragœdia :*
> ———— *et movit pictis immixa cothurnis*
> *Densum cesarie terque quaterque caput.*

Her heyre rudely disheveled, her chaplet withered, her visage with teares stayned, her brow furrowed, her eyes dejected, nay, her whole complexion quite faded and altered; and, perusing her habit, I might behold the colour of her fresh roabe all crimson breathed, and with the envenomed juice of some profane spilt inke in every place stained; nay more, her busken of all the wonted jewels and ornaments utterly despoyled, about which, in manner of a garter, I might behold these letters, written in a playne and large character :

> Behold my tragicke buskin rent and torne,
> Which kings and emperors in their tymes have worne.

This I no sooner had perused, but suddenly I might perceave the inraged Muse cast up her skornfull head : her eyebals sparkle fire, and a suddain dash of disdaine, intermixt with rage, purples her cheeke. When, pacing with a maiesticke gate, and rowsing up her fresh spirits with a lively and queint action, shee began in these or the like words.

Grande sonant tragici, tragicos decet ira cothurnos.

Am I Melpomene, the buskend Muse,
That held in awe the tyrants of the world,
And playde their lives in publicke theaters,
Making them feare to sinne, since fearelesse I
Prepar'd to write their lives in crimson inke,
And act their shames in eye of all the world ?
Have not I whipt Vice with a scourge of steele,
Unmaskt sterne Murther, sham'd lascivious Lust,
Pluckt off the visar from grimme Treason's face,
And made the sunne point at their ugly sinnes ?
Hath not this powerful hand tam'd fiery Rage,
Kild poysonous Envy with her owne keene darts,
Choak't up the covetous mouth with moulten gold,
Burst the vast wombe of eating Gluttony,
And drown'd the Drunkard's gall in juice of grapes ?
I have showed Pryde his picture on a stage,
Layde ope the ugly shapes his steele-glasse hid,
And made him passe thence meekely. In those daies
When emperours with their presence grac't my sceanes,
And thought none worthy to present themselves
Save emperours, to delight embassadours,
Then did this garland florish, then my roabe
Was of the deepest crimson, the best dye :

Cura ducum fuerant olim regumque poetæ,
Præmiaque antiqui magna tulere chori.

Who lodge then in the bosome of great kings,
Save he that had a grave cothurnate Muse ?

A stately verse in an Iambick stile
Became a Kesar's mouth.   Oh! these were times
Fit for you bards to vent your golden rymes.
Then did I tread on arras; cloth of tissue
Hung round the fore-front of my stage; the pillers
That did support the roofe of my large frame
Double appareld in pure Ophir gold,
Whilst the round circle of my spacious orbe
Was throng'd with princes, dukes, and senators.
Nunc hedaræ sine honore jacent.
But now's the iron age, and black-mouth'd curres
Barke at the vertues of the former world.
Such with their breath have blasted my fresh roabe,
Pluckt at my flowry chaplet, towsed my tresses;
Nay, some who, for their basenesse hist and skorn'd,
The stage, as loathsome, hath long-since spued out,
Have watcht their time to cast invenom'd inke
To stayne my garments with.   Oh! Seneca,
Thou tragicke poet, hadst thou liv'd to see
This outrage done to sad Melpomene,
With such sharpe lynes thou wouldst revenge my blot,
As armed Ovid against Ibis wrot.

With that in rage shee left the place, and I my dreame, for
at the instant I awaked; when, having perused this vision over
and over againe in my remembrance, I suddenly bethought
mee, how many ancient poets, tragicke and comicke, dying
many ages agoe, live still amongst us in their works: as,
amongst the Greekes, Euripides, Menander, Sophocles, Eupolis, Æschylus, Aristophanes, Apollodorus, Anaxandrides,
Nicomachus, Alexis, Tereus, and others; so, among the
Latins, Attilius, Actius, Melithus, Plautus, Terens, and others,
whome for brevity sake I omit.

Hos ediscit, et hos arcto stipata theatro
Spectat Roma potens; habet hos, numeratque poëtas.

These potent Rome acquires and holdeth deare,
And in their round theaters flocks to heare.

These, or any of these, had they lived in the afternoone of the world, as they dyed even in the morning, I assure my selfe would have left more memorable tropheys of that learned Muse, whome, in their golden numbers, they so richly adorned. And, amongst our moderne poets, who have bene industrious in many an elaborate and ingenious poem, even they whose pennes have had the greatest trafficke with. the stage, have bene in the excuse of these Muses most forgetfull. But, leaving these, lest I make too large a head to a small body, and so mishape my subject, I will begin with the antiquity of acting comedies, tragedies, and hystories. And first in the golden world.

In the first of the Olimpiads, amongst many other active exercises in which Hercules ever triumph'd as victor, there was in his nonage presented unto him by his tutor, in the fashion of a history acted by the choyse of the nobility of Greece, the worthy and memorable acts of his father Jupiter: which being personated with lively and well spirited action, wrought such impression in his noble thoughts, that in meere emulation of his father's valor (not at the behest of his stepdame Juno), he perform'd his twelve labours. Him valiant Theseus followed, and Achilles Theseus; which bred in them such hawty and magnanimous attempts, that every succeeding age hath recorded their worths unto fresh admiration. Aristotle, that prince of philosophers, whose bookes carry such credit even in these our universities, that to say *ipse dixit* is a sufficient *axioma*, hee, having the tuition of young Alexander, caused the destruction of Troy to be acted before his pupill; in which the valor of Achilles was so naturally exprest, that it imprest the hart of Alexander, in so much that all his succeeding actions were meerly shaped after that patterne; and it may be imagined that, had Achilles never lived, Alexander had never conquered the whole world. The like assertion may be made of that ever-renowned Roman, Julius Cæsar, who, after the like representation of Alexander in the temple of Hercules, standing in Gades, was never in any peace of thoughts, till by his memorable exployts hee had purchas'd to himselfe the name of Alexander, as Alexander, till hee thought himself of desert to be called Achilles; Achilles, Theseus; Theseus, till he had sufficiently imitated the acts of Hercules; and Hercules, till hee held himselfe worthy to be called the son of Jupiter. Why should not the lives of these worthyes, presented in these our dayes, effect the like wonders in the princes of our times, which can no way bee so exquisitly demonstrated, nor so lively portrayed, as by action. Oratory is a kind of speaking picture; therefore, may some say, is it not sufficient to discourse to the eares of princes the fame of these conquerors? Painting, likewise, is a dumbe oratory; therefore may we not as well, by some curious Pygmalion, drawe their conquests to worke the like love in princes towards these worthyes, by shewing them their pictures drawn to the life, as it wrought on the poore painter to bee inamoured of his owne shadow? I answer this.

Non magis expressi vultus per ahenea signa,
Quàm per vatis opus mores animique virorum
Clarorum apparent.——

The visage is no better cut in brasse,
Nor can the carver so expresse the face,
As doth the poet's penne, whose arts surpasse
To give men's lives and vertues their due grace.

A description is only a shadow, received by the eare, but not perceived by the eye; so lively portrature is meerely a forme seene by the eye, but can neither shew action, passion, motion, or any other gesture to moove the spirits of the beholder to admiration: but to see a souldier shap'd like a souldier, walke, speake, act like a souldier; to see a Hector all besmered in blood, trampling upon the bulkes of kinges;

a Troilus returning from the field, in the sight of his father Priam, as if man and horse, even from the steed's rough fetlockes to the plume on the champion's helmet, had bene together plunged into a purple ocean; to see a Pompey ride in triumph, then a Cæsar conquer that Pompey; labouring Hannibal alive, hewing his passage through the Alpes. To see as I have seene, Hercules, in his owne shape, hunting the boare, knocking downe the bull, taming the hart, fighting with Hydra, murdering Geryon, slaughtering Diomed, wounding the Stymphalides, killing the Centaurs, pashing the lion, squeezing the dragon, dragging Cerberus in chaynes, and lastly, on his high pyramides writing *Nil ultra*, Oh, these were sights to make an Alexander!

To turne to our domesticke hystories: what English blood, seeing the person of any bold Englishman presented, and doth not hugge his fame, and hunnye at his valor, pursuing him in his enterprise with his best wishes, and as beeing wrapt in contemplation, offers to him in his hart all prosperous performance, as if the personator were the man personated? so bewitching a thing is lively and well-spirited action, that it hath power to new-mold the harts of the spectators, and fashion them to the shape of any noble and notable attempt. What coward, to see his countryman valiant, would not bee ashamed of his owne cowardise? What English prince, should hee behold the true portrature of that famous King Edward the Third, foraging France, taking so great a king captive in his owne country, quartering the English lyons with the French flower-delyce, and would not bee suddenly inflam'd with so royale a spectacle, being made apt and fit for the like atchievement. So of Henry the Fift; but not to be tedious in any thing, Ovid, in one of his poems, holds this opinion—that Romulus was the first that brought plaies into Italy, which he thus sets downe.

Primus sollicitos fecisti, Romule, ludos,
Cum juvit viduos rapta Sabina viros:

De Arte Amandi. I.   *Tunc neque marmoreo pendebant vela theatro, &c.*

Which wee English thus—

Thou, noble Romulus, first playes contrives,
To get thy widdowed souldiers Sabine wyves—
In those dayes from the marble house did wave
No saile, no silken flagge, or ensigne brave :
Then was the tragicke stage not painted red,
Or any mixed staines on pillers spred :
Then did the sceane want art, th' unready stage
Was made of grasse and earth in that rude age ;
About the which were thick-leaved branches placed,
Nor did the audients hold themselves disgraced
Of turfe and heathy sods to make their seates,
Fram'd in degrees of earth and mossy peates.
Thus plac'd in order every Roman pry'd
Into her face that sat next by his side,
And closing with her severally gan move,
The innocent Sabine women to their love :
And whilst the piper Thuscus rudely plaid,
And by thrice stamping with his foote had made
A signe unto the rest, there was a shout,
Whose shrill report pierst all the aire about.
Now at a signe of rape, given from the king,
Round through the house the lusty Romans fling,
Leaving no corner of the same unsought,
Till every one a frighted virgin caught.
Looke, as the trembling dove the eagle flyes,
Or a yong lambe when he the woolfe espyes,
So ran the poore girles, filling th'aire with skreekes,
Emptying of all the colour their pale cheekes.
One feare possest them all, but not one looke,
This teares her haire, she hath her wits forsooke,
Some sadly sit, some on their mothers call,
Some chafe, some flye, some stay, but frighted all.

Thus were the ravish'd Sabines blushing led
(Becomming shame) unto each Roman's bed:
If any striv'd against it, streight her man
Would take her on his knee (whom feare made wan)
And say, Why weep'st thou, sweet? what ailes my deere?
Dry up these drops, these clowds of sorrow cleere:
Il'e be to thee, if thou thy griefe will smother,
Such as thy father was unto thy mother.
Full well could Romulus his souldiers please,
To give them such faire mistresses as these.
If such rich wages thou wilt give to me,
Great Romulus, thy souldier I will be.

Romulus, having erected the walles of Rome and leading under him a warlike nation, being in continuall war with the Sabines, after the choyce selecting of a place fit for so famous a citty, and not knowing how to people the same, his traine wholly consisting of souldiers, who, without the company of women (they not having any in their army) could not multiply, but so were likely that their immortal fames should dye issulesse with their mortal bodies, thus, therefore, Romulus devised :—After a parle and attonement made with the neighbour nations, hee built a theater, plaine, according to the time, yet large, fit for the entertainement of so great an assembly; and these were they whose famous issue peopled the cittie of Rome, which in after ages grew to such height that not Troy, founded by Dardanus—Carthage, layed by Dido—Tyrus, built by Agenor—Memphis, made by Ogdous—Thebes, seated by Cadmus—nor Babylon, reared by Semiramis—were any way equal to this situation, grounded by Romulus, to which all the discovered kingdomes of the earth after became tributaries. And in the noon-tide of their glory, and height of all their honor, they edified theaters and amphi-theaters; for in their flourishing common-weale their publike comedians and tragedians most florished, insomuch that the tragicke and comicke poets were all generally admired of the people, and particularly every man of his private Mecænas.

Imperante Augusto natus est Christus. Imperante Tiberio cru- cifixus. In the reigne of Augustus, Christ was born; and, as well in his dayes as before his birth, these solemnities were held in the greatest estimation. In Julius Cæsar's time, predecessor to Augustus, the famous hony-tong'd orator, Cicero, florished; who, amongst many other his eloquent orations, writ certaine yet extant, for the comedian, Roscius *(pro Roscio Comædo)*, of whom we shall speake more large hereafter. These continued in their honour till the reigne of Tiberius Cæsar; and under Tiberius Christ was crucified. To this end do I use this assertion, because, in the full and perfect time our Saviour sojourned on the earth, even in those happy and peacefull dayes, the spacious theaters were in the greatest opinion amongst the Romans; yet neither Christ himselfe, nor any of his sanctified apostles, in any of their sermons, acts, or documents, so much as named them, or upon any abusive occasion touched them. Therefore hence (me thinkes) a very probable and important argument may be grounded, that since they in their divine wisdomes knew all the sinnes abounding in the world before that time, taxt and reproved all the abuses reigning in that time, and foresaw all the actions and inconveniences (to the church prejudiciall) in the time to come, since they (I say), in all their holy doctrines, bookes, and principles of divinity, were content to passe them over, as things tollerated and indifferent, why should any nice and over-scrupulous heads, since they cannot ground their curiousnesse either upon the Old or New Testament, take upon them to correct, controule, or carpe at that, against which they cannot finde any text in the sacred scriptures?

In the time of Nero Cæsar, the apostle Paul was persecuted and suffered—Nero was then emperour: Paul writ his Epistle to the Romans, and at the same time did the theaters most florish amongst the Romans; yet where can we quote any place in his epistles which forbids the church of God, then resident in Rome, to absent themselves from any such assemblies?

To speake my opinion with all indifferency, God hath not enjoyned us to weare all our apparrell solely to defend the cold : some garments we weare for warmth, others for ornament. So did the children of Israel hang eare-rings in their eares, nor was it by the law forbidden them. That purity is not look't for at our hands, being mortall and humane, that is required of the angels, being celestiall and divine. God made us of earth, men; knowes our natures, dispositions, and imperfections, and therefore hath limited us a time to rejoyce, as he hath enjoyned us a time to mourne for our transgressions; and I hold them more scrupulous than well advised, that go about to take from us the use of all moderate recreations. Why hath God ordained for man varietie of meates, dainties, and delicates, if not to taste thereon? Why doth the world yeeld choyce of honest pastimes, if not decently to use them? Was not the hare made to be hunted? the stagge to be chaced? and so of all other beasts of game in their severall kindes. Since God hath provided us of these pastimes, why may we not use them to his glory? Now, if you aske me why were not the theaters as gorgeously built in all other cities of Italy as Rome, and why are not play-houses maintained as well in other cities of England as London? My answere is, It is not meet every meane esquire should carry the part belonging to one of the nobility, or for a noble-man to usurpe the estate of a prince. Rome was a metropolis, a place whither all the nations knowne under the sunne resorted: so is London, and being to receive all estates, all princes, all nations, therefore to affoord them all choyce of pastimes, sports, and recreations. Yet were there theaters in all the greatest cities of the world, as we will more largely particularize hereafter.

I never yet could read any history of any commonweale, which did not thrive and prosper whilst these publike solemnities were held in adoration. Oh! but (say some) Marcus Aurelius banisht all such triviall exercises beyond the confines of Italy. Indeed, this emperour was a philosopher of the sect of Diogenes, a Cinicke; and whether the hand of Diogenes would become a scepter or a root better, I leave to your judgments. This Aurelius was a great and sharpe reprover, who, because the matrons and ladies of Rome, in scorne of his person, made a play of him, in his time interdicted the use of their theatres: so, because his wife, Faustine, plaid false with him, he generally exclaimed against all women; because himselfe could not touch an instrument, he banisht all the musitians in Rome; and, being a meere coward, put all the gladiators and sword-players into exile. And, lest his owne suspected life should be againe acted by the comedians, as it before had beene by the noble matrons, he profest himselfe adversary to all of that quality; so severe a reformation of the weale publike hee used, restraining the citizens of their free liberties, which till his daies was not scene in Rome. But what profited this the weale publicke? Do but peruse the ancient Roman chronicles, and you shall undoubtedly finde, that from the time of this precise Emperour, that stately city, whose lofty buildings crowned seven high hils at once, and over-peered them all, streight way begun to hang the head. By degrees the forreigne kingdomes revolted, and the homage done them by strange nations was in a little space quite abrogated; for they governed all the world, some under consuls, some under pro-consuls, presidents, and pretors: they divided their dominions and contryes into principalities, some into provinces, some into toparchyes, some into tetrarchyes, some into tribes, others into ethnarchyes; but now their homage ceast, Marcus Aurelius ended their mirth, which presaged, that shortly after should begin their sorrow. He banisht their liberty, and immediately followed their bondage; for Rome, which till then kept all the nations of the world in subjective awe, was in a little space awd even by the basest nations of the world.

To leave Italy and looke backe into Greece. The sages and princes of Grecia, who for the refinednesse of their language were in such reputation through the world, that all other tongues were esteemed barbarous, these, that were the first understanders, trained up their youthful nobility to bee actors, debarring the base mechanickes so worthy employment; for none but the young heroes were admitted that practise, so to embolden them in the delivery of any forraine embassy. These wise men of Greece (so called by the Oracle) could by their industry finde out no neerer or directer course to plant humanity and manners in the hearts of the multitude, then to instruct them by moralized mysteries what vices to avoyd, what vertues to embrace, what enormities to abandon, what ordinances to observe; whose lives, being for some speciall endowments in former times honoured, they should admire and follow; whose vicious actions, personated in some licentious liver, they should despise and shunne; which, borne out as well by the wisedome of the poet, as supported by the worth of the actors, wrought such impression in the hearts of the plebe, that in short space they excelled in civility and governement, insomuch that from them all the neighbour nations drew their patternes of humanity, as well in the establishing of their lawes, as the reformation of their manners. These Magi and Gymnosophistæ, that lived (as I may say) in the childhood and infancy of the world, before it knew how to speake perfectly, thought even in those dayes that action was the neerest way to plant understanding in the hearts of the ignorant. Yea, (but say some) you ought not to confound the habits of either sex, as to let your boyes weare the attires of virgins, &c. To which I answere: The scriptures are not alwayes to be expounded meerely according to the letter (for in such estate stands our mayne sacramentall controversie), but they ought exactly to bee conferred with the purpose they handle. To do as the Sodomites did, use preposterous lusts in preposterous habits, is in that text flatly and severely forbidden; nor can I imagine any man, that hath in him any taste or relish of christianity, to be guilty of so abhorred a sinne. Besides, it is not probable that playes were meant in that text, because we read not of any playes knowne, in that time that Deuteronomie was writ, among the children of Israel. Nor do I hold it lawfull to beguile the eyes of the world in confounding the shapes of either sex, as to keep any youth in the habit of a virgin, or any virgin in the shape of a lad, to shroud them from the eyes of their fathers, tutors, or protectors, or to any other sinister intent whatsoever; but, to see our youths attired in the habit of women, who knowes not what their intents be? who cannot distinguish them by their names, assuredly knowing they are but to represent such a lady, at such a time appoynted?

Do not the Universities, the fountaines and well springs of all good arts, learning, and documents, admit the like in their colledges? and they (I assure my selfe) are not ignorant of their true use. In the time of my residence in Cambridge, I have seen tragedyes, comedyes, historyes, pastorals, and shewes, publickly acted, in which the graduates of good place and reputation have bene specially parted. This it held necessary for the emboldening of their junior schollers to arme them with audacity against they come to bee employed in any publicke exercise, as in the reading of the dialecticke, rhetoricke, ethicke, mathematicke, the physicke, or metaphysike lectures. It teacheth audacity to the bashfull grammarian, beeing newly admitted into the private colledge, and, after matriculated and entred as a member of the University, and makes him a bold sophister, to argue *pro et contra* to compose his syllogysmes, cathegoricke, or hypotheticke (simple or compound), to reason and frame a sufficient argument to prove his questions, or to defend any *axioma*, to distinguish of any dilemma, and be able to moderate in any argumentation whatsoever.

To come to rhetoricke: it not onely emboldens a scholler to speake, but instructs him to speake well, and with judgement to observe his commas, colons, and full poynts; his parentheses, his breathing spaces, and distinctions; to keepe a decorum in his countenance, neither to frowne when he should smile, nor to make unseemely and disguised faces in the delivery of his words; not to stare with his eies, draw awry his mouth, confound his voice in the hollow of his throat, or teare his words hastily betwixt his teeth; neither to buffet his deske like a mad man, nor stande in his place like a livelesse image, demurely plodding, and without any smooth and formal motion. It instructs him to fit his phrases to his action, and his action to his phrase, and his pronuntiation to them both.

Tully, in his booke *Ad Caium Herennium*, requires five things in an orator—invention, disposition, eloquution, memory, and pronuntiation; yet all are imperfect without the sixt, which is action, for be his invention never so fluent and exquisite, his disposition and order never so composed and formall, his eloquence and elaborate phrases never so materiall and pithy, his memory never so firme and retentive, his pronuntiation never so musicall and plausive, yet without a comely and elegant gesture, a gratious and a bewitching kinde of action, a naturall and familiar motion of the head, the hand, the body, and a moderate and fit countenance sutable to all the rest, I hold all the rest as nothing. A delivery and sweet action is the glosse and beauty of any discourse that belongs to a scholler. And this is the action behoovefull in any that professe this quality, not to use any impudent or forced motion in any part of the body, nor rough or other violent gesture; nor on the contrary to stand like a stiffe starcht man, but to qualifie every thing according to the nature of the person personated: for in overacting trickes, and toyling too much in the anticke habit of humors, men of the ripest desert, greatest opinions, and best reputations, may breake into the most violent absurdities. I take not upon me to teach, but to advise, for it becomes my juniority rather to be pupil'd my selfe, then to instruct others.

To proceed, and to looke into those men that professe themselves adversaries to this quality, they are none of the gravest and most ancient doctors of the academy, but onely a sorte of finde-faults, such as interest their prodigall tongues in all men's affaires without respect. These I have heard as liberally in their superficiall censures taxe the exercises performed in their colledges, as these acted on our publicke stages, not looking into the true and direct use of either, but ambitiously preferring their owne presumptuous humors, before the profound and authenticall judgements of all the learned doctors of the Universitie. Thus you see, that touching the antiquity of actors and acting, they have not beene new, lately begot by any upstart invention, but I have derived them from the first Olimpiads, and I shall continue the use of them even till this present age. And so much touching their antiquity.

Pars superest cœpti : pars est exhausta laboris.

THE END OF THE FIRST BOOKE.

OF ACTORS, AND

their ancient Dignitie.

THE SECOND BOOKE.

JULIUS CÆSAR, the famous conquerour, discoursing with Marcus Cicero, the as famous orator, amongst many other matters debated it pleased the emperour to aske his opinion of the *histriones*, the players of Rome, pretending some cavell against them, as men whose imployment in the common-weale was unnecessary. To whom Cicero answered thus: Content thee, Cæsar: there bee many heads busied and bewitched with these pastimes now in Rome, which otherwise would be inquisitive after thee and thy greatnesse. Which answere, how sufficiently the emperour approved, may be conjectured by the many guifts bestowed, and priviledges and charters after granted to men of that quality. Such was likewise the opinion of a great statesman of this land, about the time that certaine bookes were called in question. Doubtlesse there be many men of that temper, who, were they not carried away, and weaned from their owne corrupt and bad disposition, and by accidentall meanes removed and altered from their dangerous and sullen intendments, would be found apt and prone to many notorious and trayterous practises. Kings and monarches are by God placed and inthroaned *supra nos*, above us, and we are to regard them as the sun from whom we receive the light to live under, whose beauty and brightnesse we may onely admire, not meddle with. *Ne ludamus cum Diis:* they that shoot at the starres over their heads, their arrowes fall directly downe, and wound themselves. But this allusion may be better referred to the use of action promised in our third treatise, then to their dignity, which next and immediately (by God's grace) our purpose is to handle.

The word *tragedy* is derived from the Greeke word τράγος, *caper*, a goat, because the goat, being a beast most injurious to the vines, was sacrificed to Bacchus. Heereupon Diodurus writes that tragedies had their first names from the oblations due to Bacchus; or else of τρὺξ, a kinde of painting, which the tragedians of the old time used to stayne their faces with. By the censure of Horace, Thespis was the first tragicke writer:

Horace, Arte Poeticâ.

Ignotum tragicæ genus invenisse camenæ
Dicitur, et plaustris vexisse poëmata Thespis.

The unknowne Tragicke Muse Thespis first sought,
And her high poems in her chariot brought.

This Thespis was an Athenian poet, borne in Thespina, a free towne in Bœotia by Helicon: of him the nine Muses were called Thespiades. But by the censure of Quintilian, Æschylus was before him; but after them Sophocles and Euripides clothed their tragedies in better ornament. Livius

Potid. Virgil.

Andronicus was the first that writ any Roman tragedy, in which kinde of poësie Accius, Pacuvius, Seneca, and Ovidius excelled.

Ovid, Amo-rum. lib. 2. Eleg. 18.

Sceptra tamen sumpsi: curáque tragædia nostra
Crevit; at huic operi quamlibet aptus eram.

The sceptred tragedy then proov'd our wit,
And to that worke we found us apt and fit.

Againe, in his fift Booke, *De tristibus. Eleg.* 8.

Carmina quòd vestro saltari nostra theatro
Versibus, et plaudi scribis (amice) meis.

Deere friend, thou writ'st our Muse is 'mongst you song,
And in your theaters with plaudits rong.

Likewise in his epistle to Augustus, writ from the Ponticke Island, whither he was banisht:

Et dedimus tragicis scriptum regale cothurnis,
Quæque gravis debet verba cothurnus habet.

With royall stile speakes our Cothurnate Muse,
A buskind phrase in buskin'd playes we use.

The word *comedy* is derived from the Greeke word Κόμος, a street, and ῷδη, *cantus*, a street song; as signifying there was ever mirth in those streets where Comedies most florisht:

Hæc paces habuere bonæ, ventique secundi.

In this kind, Aristophanes, Eupolis, Cratinus were famous; after them, Menander and Philemon: succeeding them, Cicilius, Nævius, Plautus, and Terentius.

Musaque Turani tragicis innixa cothurnis
Et tua cum socco, Musa, Melisse levis.

Turanus' tragicke buskin grac'd the play,
Melissa's comicke shooe made lighter way.

The ancient histriographers write, that among the Greekes there were divers places of exercises *Alex. Metapol.* appointed for poets; some at the grave of Theseus, others at Helicon, where they in comedies and tragedies contended for several prises, where Sophocles was ajudged victor over Æschylus. There were others in the citty of Elis, where Menander was foyled by Philemon. In the same kinde, Hesiod is sayd to have triumpht over Homer. So Corinna, (for her excellencies in these inventions, called *musica lyrica*) excelled Pindarus, the Theban poet, for which she was five times crowned with garlands.

The first publicke theater was by Dionysius built in Athens: it was fashioned in the manner of a semi-circle, or halfe-moone, whose galleries and degrees were reared from the ground, their staires high, in the midst of which did arise the stage, beside, such a convenient distance from the earth, that the audience assembled might easily behold the whole project without impediment. From this the Romanes had their first patterne, which at the first not being roof't, but lying open to all weathers, Quintus Catulus was the first that caused the outside to bee covered with linnen cloth, and the inside to bee hung round with curtens of silke. But when Marcus Scaurus was Ædilis, hee repaired it, and supported it round with pillers of marble.

Caius Curio, at the solemne obsequies of his father, erected a famous theater of timber, in so strange a forme that, on two several stages, two sundry playes might be acted at once, and yet the one bee no hinderance or impediment to the other; and, when hee so pleased, the whole frame was artificially composed to meet in the middest, which made an amphi-theater.

Pompey the great, after his victories against Mithridates, king of Pontus, saw in the citty Mitilene a theater of another forme; and, after his triumphes and returne to Rome, he raised one after the same patterne of free-stone, of that vast-nesse and receit, that within his spaciousnesse it was able at once to receive fourescore thousand people, every one to sit, see, and heare.

In emulation of this sumptuous and gorgious building, Julius Cæsar, successor to Pompey's greatnesse, exceeded him in his famous architecture: hee raised an amphitheater *Campo Martio*, in the field of Mars, which as farre excelled Pompey's, as Pompey's did exceed Caius Curio's, Curio's that of Marcus Scaurus, Scaurus' that of Quintus Catulus, or Ca-tulus' that which was first made in Athens by Dionysius: for the basses, columnes, pillars, and pyramides were all of hewed marble; the covering of the stage, which wee call the heavens (where upon any occasion their gods descended), were geo-metrically supported by a giant-like Atlas, whom the poets for his astrology feigne to beare heaven on his shoulders; in which an artificiall sunne and moone, of extraordinary aspect and brightnesse, had their diurnall and nocturnall motions; so had the starres their true and cœlestiall course; so had the spheares, which in their continuall motion made a most sweet and ravishing harmony. Here were the elements and planets in their degrees, the sky of the moone, the sky of Mercury, Venus, Sol, Mars, Jupiter, and Saturne; the starres, both fixed and wandering, and above all these, the first mover or *primum mobile*, there were the 12 signes; the lines equinoctiall and zodiacal; the meridian circle, or zenith; the orizon circle, or emisphere; the zones, torrid and frozen; the poles, articke and antarticke, with all other tropickes, orbs, lines, circles, the solstitium, and all other motions of the stars, signes, and planets. In briefe, in that little compasse were comprehended the perfect modell of the firmament, the whole frame of the heavens, with all grounds of astronomicall conjecture. From the roofe grew a loover, or turret, of an exceeding altitude, from which an ensigne of silke waved continually, *pendebant vela theatro.* But lest I waste too much of that compendiousnesse I have promised in my discourse in idle descriptions, I leave you to judge the proportion of the body by the making of this one limbe, every piller, seat, footpost, staire, gallery, and whatsoever else belongs to the furnishing of such a place, being in cost, substance, forme, and artificiall workmanship most sutable. The floore, stage, roofe, outside, and inside as costly as the Pantheon or Capitol. In the principall galleries were special, remote, selected, and chosen seats for the emperour, *patres conscripti*, dictators, consuls, prætors, tribunes, triumviri, decemviri, ædiles, curules, and other noble officers among the senators: all other roomes were free for the plebe, or multitude. To this purpose I introduce these famous edifices, as wondring at their cost and state, thus intimating, that if the quality of acting were (as some propose) altogether unworthy, why for the speciall practise, and memorable imployment of the same, were founded so many rare and admirable monuments? and by whom were they erected? but by the greatest princes of their times, and the most famous and worthiest of them all, builded by him that was the greatest prince of the world, Julius Cæsar, at what time in his hand he grip't the universal empire of the earth. So of Augustus Cæsar:

> *Inspice ludorum sumptus, Auguste, tuorum*
> *Empta tibi magno.*

> Behold, Augustus, the great pompe and state,
> Of these thy playes payd deere for, at hye rate.

> *Hæc tu spectasti, spectandaque sæpe dedisti.*

And could any inferiour quality bee more worthily esteemed or nobler graced, then to have princes of such magnificence and state to bestow on them places of such port and countenance? had they been never well regarded, they had been never so sufficiently provided for, nor would such worthy princes have strived who should (by their greatest expence and provision) have done them the amplest dignity, had they not with incredible favour regarded the quality. I will not traverse this too farre, least I incurre some suspition of selfe-love: I rather leave it to the favourable consideration of the wise, though to the perversenesse of the ignorant; who, had they any taste either of poesie, phylosophy, or historicall antiquity, would rather stand mated at their owne impudent ignorance, then against such noble and notable examples stand in publicke defiance.

I read of a theater built in the midst of the river Tiber, standing on pillers and arches, the foundation wrought under water like London-bridge: the nobles and ladyes, in their barges and gondelayes, landed at the very stayres of the galleryes. After these they composed others, but differing in forme from the theater, or amphitheater, and every such was called *Circus*, the frame globe-like and merely round :

Circus in hanc exit clamataque palma theatris.

And the yeare from the first building of Rome, five hundred threescore and seven, what time Spurius Posthumus Albinus, and Quintus Martius Philippus were consuls, Nero made one, and the noble Flaminius another ; but the greatest was founded by Tarquinius Priscus, and was called *Circus Maximus.* In this the gladiators practised, the widenesse and spaciousnesse was such, that in it they fought at barriers, and many times ran at tilt. Dion records eighteene elephants slaine at once in one theater. More particularly to survey the rarer monuments of Rome, neere to the Pantheon (the temple of the Roman gods), at the discent from the hil Capitolinus, lies the great Forum, by which is scituate the great amphitheater of Titus, first erected by Vespatian, but after (almost ruined by fire) by the Roman Titus rarely re-edified. It is called *Colliseus,* also a *Cavea,* which signifies a *Ammianus. lib.* 29. scaffold, also *Arena,* a place of combate, by Silvianus and Prudentius ; which name Tertullian, Pliny, Ovid, Firmicus, and Apuleius likewise give it. It had the title of *Circus, Cavea,* and *Stadium,* by Suetonius, Capitolinus, and Arcadius. Cassianus affirmes these theaters consecrated to Diana Taurica, Tertullian to Mars and Diana, Martial to Jupiter Latiaris, and to Stygian Pluto, whose opinion Minutius and Prudentius approve. The first structures were by the tribune Curio, which Dio, lib. 37, affirmes. Vitruvius, lib. 5, saith, *Multa theatra Romæ structa quot* *Pliny. lib.* 36. *annis.* Of Julius Cæsar's amphitheater *Campo Martio* Dio Cassius records, which Augustus *Dio Cassius. lib.* 43. after patronized, as Victor remembers of them, whose charge Statilius Taurus assisted, of whom *Dio* speaketh thus — Ὁ ταῦρος Στατίλιος θέατρον, &c. *anno urbis* *Dio. lib.* 51. DCCXXV. Pub. Victor forgets not *Circus Flamminii,* and Sue-

Suetonius. cap. 21.

Tacitus. lib. 13. *Annalium.*

tonius remembers one builded by Caligula at Septa, whose building Claudius at first interdicted. Nero erected a magnificent theater in the field of Mars. Suetonius, lib. *Ner.* 12.

Publius Victor speakes further of a *castrense theatrum,* a theater belonging to the campe in the country of the Æsquiles, built by Tiberius Cæsar, and of Pompey's theater Pliny witnesseth.

Pliny. lib. 36, *cap.* 15.

The great theater of Statilius, being in greatest use, was burnt in the time of Nero, which Xiphilinus thus speakes of, τό τε παλατιον τὸ ὄρος σύμπαν κὰι τὸ θέατρον τὸν Ταύρου ἐκαύθη· This was built in the middest of the old citty, and after the combustion repaired by Vespatian, *Consulatu suo* 8, whose coyne of one side beares the express figure of his theater ; yet was it onely begun by him, but perfected by his sonne Titus. Eutropius and Cassiodorus attribute this place soly to Titus, but Aurelius Victor gives him onely the honour of the perfecting a place so exquisitely begun : this after was repaired by Marcus Anthonius Pius, by whose cost, sayth Capitolinus, the temple of Hadrianus was repaired, and the great theater reedified, which Heliogabalus, by the testimony of Lampridius, patronized, and after the senate of Rome tooke to their protection under the Gordians.

Touching theaters without Rome, Lypsius records *Theatra circà Romam extructa passim :* even in Jerusalem, *Herodes magnificus et illustris rex non uno loco Judeæ amphi-theatra edificavit, extruxit in ipsá urbe sacrá,* ἐν τῷ πηδιῳ (as Josephus saith) Ἀμφιθέατρον μέγιστον. Herod, a magnificent and illustrious king, not in one place of Judea erected amphitheaters, but even in the holy citty hee built one of greatest receit. Also in Greece, Asia, Africke, Spaine, France ; nor is there any province in which their ancient structures do not yet remaine, or their perishing ruines are not still remembered. In Italy *ad Lirim, Campaniæ fluvium juxta Minturnas* remaines part of an ample amphi-theater.

At Puteolis, a city by the sea-side in Campania, 8 miles from Naples, one.

At Capua, a magnificent one of sollid marble.

At Alba, in Italy, one.

At Ocrioulum, in Umbria, one.

At Verona, one most beautiful.

At Florence, one whose compasse yet remaines.

At Athens, in Greece, one of marble.

At Pola, in Istria, by the Hadriaticke sea, one described by Sebastian Serlius.

At Hyspalis, in Spaine, one built without the walles of the citty.

In Turamace, in Vesuna, one of squared stone, the length of 30 perches, or poles, the breadth 20.

At Arelate one.

At Burdegall, one.

At Nemaus, one, remembred by Euseb. in Ecclesiastica Historia.

At Lygeris, one.

Another among the Helvetians.

The *Veronense theatrum marmoreum*, erected before the time of Augustus, as Torellus Serayna in his description of Verona records, but Cyrnicus Anconitanus reports it built in the nine and thirtieth yeare of Octavian : Carolus Sigonius referres it to the reigne of Maximinian, who saith Maximinian built theaters in Mediolanum, Aquilea, and Brixium. The like Cornelius Tacitus, 2 *Hist.*, *Sicon, lib. Hist. Occident.* remembers in Placentia, but the description of the Verona theater Levinus Kersmakerus sets downe. This the great king Francis, *anno* 1539, gave to certain actors, who thirty dayes space together represented in the same the Acts of the Apostles, nor was it lawfull by the edict of the king for any man to remove any stone within thirty poles of his scituation, lest they should endanger the foundation of the theater.

The like have been in Venice, Millan, Padua. In Paris

there are divers now in use by the French king's comedians, as the Burgonian, and others. Others in Massilia, in Trevers, Magontia, in Agrippina, and infinite cities of Greece, Thebes, Carthage, Delphos, Crete, Paphos, Epirus, also in the citie of Tydena, so at Civil, in Spaine, and at Madrill, with others.

Archduke Alphonsus.   At the entertainement of the Cardinall Alphonsus and the infant of Spaine in the Low-countryes, they were presented at Antwerpe with sundry pageants and playes : the King of Denmarke, father to him that now reigneth, entertained into his service a company of English comedians, commended unto him by the honourable the Earle of Leicester : the Duke of Brunswicke and the Landgrave of Hessen retaine in their courts certaine of ours of the same quality. But among the Romans they were in highest reputation, for in comparison of their playes they never regarded any of their solemnities, there *ludi funebres*, there *Floralia, Cerealia, Frugalia, Bacchanalia*, or *Lupercalia.*

Stowe.   And amongst us one of our best English Chroniclers records, that when Edward the Fourth would shew himselfe in publicke state to the view of the people, hee repaired to his palace at S. Johnes, where he accustomed to see the citty actors : and since then that house, by the prince's free gift, hath belonged to the Office of the Revels, where our court playes have beene in late daies yearely rehersed, perfected, and corrected before they come to the publike view of the prince and the nobility. Ovid, speaking of the Tragicke Muse, thus writes.

> *Venit et ingenti violenta tragedia passu,*
> *Fronte comæ torvá palla jacebat humi :*
> *Læva manus sceptrum laté regale tenebat,*
> *Lydius apta pedum vincta cothurnus habet.*

> Then came the Tragicke Muse with a proud pace,
> Measuring her slow strides with majesticke grace :

Her long traine sweepes the earth, and she doth stand
With buskin'd legge, rough brow, and sceptred hand.

Well knew the poet what estimation she was in with Augustus, when he describes her holding in her left hand a scepter. Now to recite some famous actors that lived in the preceding ages. The first comedians were Cincius and Faliscus; the first tragedians were Minutius and Prothonius. Ælius Donatus, in his preface to Terence his Andria, saith that in *Cincius.* that comedy Lucius Attilius, Latinus Prænes- *Faliscus.* *Minutius.* tinus, and Lucius Ambivius Turpio were actors: *Prothonius.* this comedy was dedicated to Cibil, and such *L. Attilius.* *Latinus* were called *Ludi Megalenses*, acted in the yeare *Prænestinus.* that M. Fulvius was Ædilis, Quintus Minutius *Lucius* *Ambivius* Valerius, and M. Glabrio were Curules, which *Turpio.* were counsellers and chiefe officers in Rome, so called because they customably sate in chayres of ivory. The songs that were sung in this comedy were set by Flaccus, the *Flaccus.* sonne of Clodius. Terence his Eunuchus, or Second Comedy, was acted in the yeare L. Posthumus and L. Cornelius were Ædil. Curules, Marcus Valerius, and Caius Fannius Consuls. The yeare from the building *Protinus.* of Rome, 291, in his Adelphi one Protinus acted *L. Servius.* and was highly applauded, in his Hecyra Julius *Offic. I.* Servius. Cicero commends one Rupilius, a rare tragedian. I read of another called Arossus, another called Theocrines, who purchased him a great applause *Rupilius.* in the playes called Terentini. There were other *Arossus.* *Theocrines.* playes in Rome, called Actia and Pythia, made in *Æsopus.* honour of Apollo for killing the dragon Python. In those one Æsopus bare the praise, a man generally esteemed, who left behind him much substance, which Clodius, his sonne, after possest.

Quæ gravis Æsopus, quæ doctus Roscius egit.

Labericus.   Labericus was an excellent poet and a rare actor, who writ a booke of the gesture and action to be used by the tragedians and comedians in performance of every part in his native humor. Plautus himselfe was so inamored of the actors in his dayes, that hee published many excellent and *Theodoretes.* exquisite comedies yet extant. Aristotle commends one Theodoretes to be the best tragedian in his time. This in the presence of Alexander personated Achilles, which so delighted the emperour that hee bestowed on him a pension of *quinque mille drachmæ*, five thousand drachmaes, and every thousand drachmaes are twenty nine pounds, three shillings, foure pence sterling.

Roscius, whom the eloquent orator and excellent statesman of Rome, Marcus Cicero, for his elegant pronuntiation and formall gesture called his jewell, had from the common treasury of the Roman Exchequer a daily pention allowed him of so many *sestertii* as in our coine amount to 16 pound and a marke, or thereabouts, which yearely did arise to any noblemans revenues. So great was the fame of this Roscius, and so good his estimation, that learned Cato made a question whether Cicero could write better then Roscius could speake and act, or Roscius speake and act better then Cicero write? Many times, when they had any important orations to be with an audible and loud voyce delivered to the people, they imployed the tongue and memory of this excellent actor, to whom for his worth the senate granted such large exhibition.

> *quæ pervincere voces*
> *Evaluere sonum, referunt quem nostra theatra?*
> *Garganum mugire putes nemus, aut mare Thuscum ;*
> *Tanto cum strepitu ludi spectantur et artes.*

What voyce can be compared with the sound
Our theaters from their deepe concaves send ?
For their reverberate murmurs seeme to drownd
The Gorgan wood, when the proud windes contend,

Or when rough stormes the Thuscan billowes raise ;
With such loud joy they ring our arts and playes.

To omit all the doctors, zawnyes, pantaloones, harlakeenes, in which the French, but especially the Italians, have beene excellent, and according to the occasion offered to do some right to our English actors, as Knell, Bentley, Mils, Wilson, Crosse, Lanam, and others, these, since I never saw them, as being before my time, I cannot (as an eye-witnesse of their desert) give them that applause, which no doubt they worthily merit ; yet by the report of many juditiall auditors their performances of many parts have been so absolute, that it were a kinde of sinne to drowne their worths in Lethe, and not commit their (almost forgotten) names to eternity. Here I must needs remember Tarleton, in his time gratious with the queene, his soveraigne, and in the people's generall applause, whom succeeded Wil. Kemp, as wel in the favour of her majesty, as in the opinion and good thoughts of the generall audience. Gabriel, Singer, Pope, Phillips, Sly, all the right I can do them is but this, that, though they be dead, their deserts yet live in the remembrance of many. Among so many dead, let me not forget one yet alive, in his time the most worthy, famous Maister Edward Allen. To omit these, as also such as for their divers imperfections may be thought insufficient for the quality, actors should be men pick'd out personable, according to the parts they present : they should be rather schollers, that, though they cannot speake well, know how to speake, or else to have that volubility that they can speake well, though they understand not what, and so both imperfections may by instructions be helped and amended : but where a good tongue and a good conceit both faile, there can never be good actor. I also could wish, that such as are condemned for their licentiousnesse, might by a generall consent bee quite excluded our society ; for, as we are men that stand in the broad eye of the world, so should our manners, gestures, and behaviours, savour of such government and modesty, to deserve the good thoughts and reports of all men, and to abide the sharpest censures even of those that are the greatest opposites to the quality. Many amongst us I know to be of substance, of government, of sober lives, and temperate carriages, house-keepers, and contributory to all duties enjoyned them, equally with them that are rank't with the most bountifull; and if amongst so many of sort, there be any few degenerate from the rest in that good demeanor which is both requisite and expected at their hands, let me entreat you not to censure hardly of all for the misdeeds of some, but rather to excuse us, as Ovid doth the generality of women:

> *Parcite paucarum diffundere crimen in omnes:*
> *Spectetur meritis quæque puella suis.*

> For some offenders, that perhaps are few,
> Spare in your thoughts to censure all the crew:
> Since every breast contains a sundry spirit,
> Let every one be censur'd as they merit.

Others there are of whom, should you aske my opinion, I must refer you to this, *Consule theatrum.* Here I might take fit opportunity to reckon up all our English writers, and compare them with the Greeke, French, Italian, and Latine poets, not only in their pastorall, historicall, elegiacall, and heroicall poems, but in their tragicall and comicall subjects; but it was my chance to happen on the like, learnedly done by an approved good scholler, in a booke called Wits Commonwealth, to which treatise I wholy referre you, returning to our present subject. Julius Cæsar himselfe for his pleasure became an actor, being in shape, state, voyce, judgement, and all other occurrents, exterior and interior, excellent. Amongst many other parts acted by him in person, it is recorded of him that, with generall applause in his own theater, he played *Hercules Furens*; and, amongst many other arguments of his compleatenesse, excellence, and extraordinary care in his action, it is thus reported of him :—Being in the depth of a passion, one of his servants (as his part then fell out) presenting Lychas, who before had from Dejanira brought him the poysoned shirt, dipt in the blood of the centaure, Nessus, he, in the middest of his torture and fury, finding this Lychas hid in a remote corner (appoynted him to creep into of purpose), although he was, as our tragedians use, but seemingly to kill him by some false imagined wound, yet was Cæsar so extremely carried away with the violence of his practised fury, and by the perfect shape of the madnesse of Hercules, to which he had fashioned all his active spirits, that he slew him dead at his foot, and after swoong him, *terque quaterque* (as the poet says) about his head. It was the manner of their emperours, in those dayes, in their publicke tragedies, to choose out the fittest amongst such as for capital offences were condemned to dye, and imploy them in such parts as were to be kild in the tragedy ; who of themselves would make suit rather so to dye with resolution, and by the hands of such princely actors, then otherwise to suffer a shamefull and most detestable end. And these were tragedies naturally performed; and such Caius Caligula, Claudius Nero, Vitellius, Domitianus, Commodus, and other emperours of Rome, upon their festivals and holy daies of greatest consecration, used to act. Therefore M. Kid, in his Spanish Tragedy, upon occasion presenting itselfe, thus writes.

> Why, Nero thought it no disparagement,
> And kings and emperours have tane delight
> To make experience of their wits in playes.

These exercises, as traditions, have beene since (though in better manner) continued through all ages, amongst all the noblest nations of the earth. But I have promised to be altogether compendious : presuming that what before is discourst may, for the practise of playes, their Antiquity and Dignity, be altogether sufficient, I omit the shewes and ceremonies, even in these times, generally used among the Catholikes, in which, by the churchmen and most religious, divers pageants, as of the Nativity, Passion, and Ascention, with other historicall places of the bible, are at divers times and seasons of the yeare usually celebrated—*sed hæc præter me.* In the yeare of the world, 4207, of Christ, 246, Origen writ certaine godly epistles to Philip, then emperour of Rome, who was the first Christian emperour, and in his life I reade that in the fourth yeare of his reigne, which was the 1000 yeare after the building of Rome, he solemnized that yeare as a jubilee with sumptuous pageants and playes. Homer, the most excellent of all poets, composed his Iliads in the shape of a tragedy, his Odisseas like a comedy. Virgil, in the first of his Æneids, in his description of Dido's Carthage,

> —————————*hic alta theatris*
> *Fundamenta locant alii, immanesque columnas*
> *Rupibus excidunt, scenis decora alta futuris.*

Which proves that in those dayes, immediately after the ruine of Troy, when Carthage had her first foundation, they built theatres with stately columnes of stone, as in his description may appeare. I have sufficiently discourst of the first theaters, and in whose times they were erected, even till the reigne of Julius Cæsar, the first emperour, and how they continued in their glory from him till the reigne of Marcus Aurelius, the 23 emperour, and from him even to these times. Now, to prove they were in as high estimation at Lacedæmon and Athens, two the most famous cities of Greece. Cicero, in his booke, *Cato Major, seu de Senectute : Cum Athenis ludis quidam grandis natu in theatrum venisset,* &c. An ancient citizen comming into one of the Athenian theatres to see the pastimes there solemnized (which shewes that the most antient and grave frequented them), by reason of the throng, no man gave him place or reverence ; but the same citizen, being imploy'd in an embassy to Lacedæmon, and coming like a private man into the theater, the generall multitude arose at once, and with great ceremonious reverence gave his age place. This Cicero alledges to prove the reverence due to age, and this I may fitly introduce to the approbation of my present subject. Moreover, this great statesman of Rome, at whose exile twenty thousand of the chiefest Roman citizens wore mourning apparrel, oftentimes commends Plautus, calling him *Plautus noster*, and *Atticorum antiqua comedia*, where he proceeds further to extoll Æsopus for personating Ajax, and the famous actor, Rupilius, in Epigonus, Medea, Menalip, Clytemnestra, and Antiope, proceeding in the same place with this worthy and grave sentence, *Ergo histrio hoc videbit in scená, quod non videbit sapiens in vitá ?*—Shall a tragedian see that in his scene, which a wise man cannot see in the course of his life? So, in another of his workes, amongst many instructions to his sonne Marcus, he applauds Turpio Ambivius for his action, Statius, Nævius, and Plautus, for their writing. Ovid *in Augustum :*

> *Luminibusque tuis totus quibus utitur orbis,*
> *Scenica vidisti lusus adulteria.*

> Those eyes, with which you all the world survey,
> See in your theaters our actors play.

Augustus Cæsar, because he would have some memory of his love to those places of pastime, reared in Rome two stately *obelisci* ,or pyramides, one in Julius Cæsar's temple in the field of Mars, another in the great theater, called *Circus Maximus*, built by Flaminius : these were in height an hundred cubits a peece, in bredth foure cubits : they were first raised by king Pheron in the temple of the Sunne, and after removed to Rome by Augustus. The occasion of their first composure was this : Pheron, for some great crime committed by him in his youth against the Gods, was by them strooke blinde, and so continued the space of ten yeares ; but, after a revelation in the citty Bucis, it was told that if he washt his eyes in the water of a woman that was chaste, and never adulterately touch't with any save her husband, he should againe recover his sight. The king first tride his wife, then many other of the most grave and best reputed matrons, but continued still in despaire, till at length hee met with one vertuous lady, by whose chastity his sight was restored, whom (having first commanded his queene and the rest to be consumed with fire) he after married. Pheron, in memory of this, builded his two pyramides, after removed to Rome by Augustus.

Sanctaque majestas, et erat venerabile nomen
Vatibus————

THE END OF THE SECOND BOOKE.

O F   A C T O R S ,   A N D

the true use of their quality.

THE THIRD BOOKE.

TRAGEDIES and comedies, saith Donatus, had their beginning *a rebus divinis,* from divine sacrifices. They differ thus : in comedies *turbulenta prima, tranquilla ultima;* in tragedyes, *tranquilla prima, turbulenta ultima:* comedies begin in trouble and end in peace ; tragedies begin in calmes, and end in tempest. Of comedies there be three kindes—moving comedies, called *motariæ;* standing comedies, called *statariæ,* or mixt betwixt both, called *mistæ:* they are distributed into foure parts, the *prologue,* that is, the preface; the *protasis,* that is the proposition, which includes the first act, and presents the actors; the *epitasis,* which is the businesse and body of the comedy; the last, the *catastrophe,* and conclusion. The deffinition of the comedy, according to the Latins : a discourse, consisting of divers institutions, comprehending civill and domesticke things, in which is taught what in our lives and manners is to be followed, what to bee avoyded. The Greekes define it thus : Κωμῳδία ἔστιν ἰδιωτικῶν καὶ πολιτικῶν πραγμάτων ἀχιν δονος ποροιχην. Cicero saith a comedy is the imitation of life, the glasse of custome, and the image of truth. In Athens they had their first originall. The ancient comedians used to attire their actors thus : the old men in white, as the most ancient of all, the yong men in party-coloured garments, to note their diversity of thoughts, their slaves and servants in thin and bare vesture, either to note their poverty, or that they might run the more lighter about their affaires : their parasites wore robes that were turned in, and intricately wrapped about them ; the fortunate in white, the discontented in decayed vesture, or garments growne out of fashion ; the rich in purple, the poore in crimson ; souldiers wore purple jackets, hand-maids the habits of strange virgins, bawds pide coates, and curtezans garments of the colour of mud, to denote their covetousnesse : the stages were hung with rich arras, which was first brought from King Attalus into Rome ; his state hangings were so costly, that from him all tapestries and rich arras were called *Attalia.* This being a thing antient, as I have proved it, next of dignity. As many arguments have confirmed it, and now even in these dayes by the best, without exception, favourably tollerated, why should I yeeld my censure, grounded on such firm and establisht sufficiency, to any tower founded on sand, any castle built in the aire, or any triviall upstart, and meere imaginary opinion ?

Oderunt hilarem tristes, tristemque jocosi.

I hope there is no man of so unsensible a spirit, that can inveigh against the true and direct use of this quality. Oh, but say they, the Romanes in their time, and some in these dayes, have abused it, and therefore we volly out our exclamations against the use. Oh shallow ! because such a man hath his house burnt, we shall quite condemne the use of fire ; because one man quaft poyson, we must forbeare to drinke ; because some have bean shipwrak't, no man shall hereafter trafficke by sea. Then I may as well argue thus : he cut his finger, therefore must I weare no knife ; yond man fell from his horse, therefore must I travell a foot ; that man surfeited, therefore I dare not eate. What can appeare more absurd then such a grosse and sencelesse assertion ? I could turne this unpoynted weapon against his breast that aimes it at mine, and reason thus : Roscius had a large pension allowed him by the senate of Rome, why should not an actor of the like desert have the like allowance now? or this, the most famous city and nation in the world held playes in great admiration; *ergo*—but it is a rule in logicke, *ex particularibus nihil fit.* These are not the basses we must build upon, nor the columnes that must support our architecture.

> *Et latro, et cautus precingitur ense viator :*
> *Ille sed insidias, hic sibi portat opem.*

> Both theeves and true-men weapons weare alike :
> Th' one to defend, the other comes to strike.

Let us use fire to warme us, not to scortch us; to make ready our necessaries, not to burne our houses : let us drinke to quench our thirst, not to surfet; and eate to satisfie nature, not to gormondize.

> *Comædiu rectá si mente legatur,*
> *Constabit nulli posse nocere.*

> Playes are in use as they are understood,
> Spectators eyes may make them bad or good.

Shall we condemne a generallity for any one particular mis-construction? give me then leave to argue thus. Amongst kings have there not beene some tyrants? yet the office of a king is the image of the majesty of God. Amongst true subjects have there not crept in some false traitors? even amongst the twelve there was Judas, but shall we for his fault censure worse of the eleven? God forbid ! art thou prince or peasant? art thou of the nobility or commonalty? Art thou merchant or souldier? of the citty or country? Art thou preacher or auditor? Art thou tutor or pupill? There have beene of thy function bad and good, prophane and holy. I induce these instances to confirme this common argument, that the use of any generall thing is not for any one particular abuse to be condemned; for if that assertion stoode firme, wee should run into many notable inconveniences.

Qui locus est templis angustior hanc quoque vitet,
In culpam si qua est ingeniosa suam.

To proceed to the matter. First, playing is an ornament to the citty, which strangers of all nations repairing hither report of in their countries, beholding them here with some admiration; for what variety of entertainment can there be in any citty of christendome more then in London? But some will say, this dish might be very well spared out of the banquet: to him I answere, Diogenes, that used to feede on rootes, cannot relish a march-pane. Secondly, our English tongue, which hath ben the most harsh, uneven, and broken language of the world, part Dutch, part Irish, Saxon, Scotch, Welsh, and indeed a gallimaffry of many, but perfect in none, is now by this secondary meanes of playing continually refined, every writer striving in himselfe to adde a new florish unto it; so that in processe, from the most rude and unpolisht tongue, it is growne to a most perfect and composed language, and many excellent workes and elaborate poems writ in the same, that many nations grow inamored of our tongue (before despised.) Neither Saphicke, Ionicke, Iambicke, Phaleuticke, Adonicke, Gliconicke, Hexamiter, Tetramitrer, Pentamiter, Asclepediacke, Choriambicke, nor any other measured verse used among the Greekes, Latins, Italians, French, Dutch, or Spanish writers, but may be exprest in English, be it blanke verse or meeter, in distichon, or hexastichon, or in what forme or feet, or what number you can desire. Thus you see to what excellency our refined English is brought, that in these daies we are ashamed of that euphony and eloquence, which within these 60 yeares the best tongues in the land were proud to pronounce. Thirdly, playes have made the ignorant more apprehensive, taught the unlearned the knowledge of many famous histories, instructed such as cannot reade in the discovery of all our English chronicles; and what man have you now of that weake capacity that cannot discourse of any notable thing recorded even from William the Conquerour, nay, from the landing of Brute, untill this day ? beeing possest of their true use, for or because playes are writ with this ayme, and carryed with this methode, to teach their subjects obedience to their king, to shew the people the untimely ends of such as have moved tumults, commotions, and insurrections, to present them with the flourishing estate of such as live in obedience, exhorting them to allegeance, dehorting them from all trayterous and fellonious stratagems.

Use of tragedies.

Omne genus scripti gravitate tragedia vincit.

If we present a tragedy, we include the fatall and abortive ends of such as commit notorious murders, which is aggravated and acted with all the art that may be to terrifie men from the like abhorred practises. If wee present a forreigne history, the subject is so intended, that in the lives of Romans, Grecians, or others, either the vertues of our countrymen are extolled, or their vices reproved; as thus, by the example of Cæsar to stir souldiers to valour and magnanimity; by the fall of Pompey that no man trust in his owne strength: we present Alexander killing his friend in his rage, to reprove rashnesse; Mydas, choked with his gold, to taxe covetousnesse; Nero against tyranny; Sardanapalus against luxury; Ninus against ambition, with infinite others, by sundry instances either animating men to noble attempts, or attacking the consciences of the spectators, finding themselves toucht in presenting the vices of others. If a morall, it is to perswade men to humanity and good life, to instruct them in civility and good manners, shewing them the fruits of honesty, and the end of villany.

Use of historicall playes.

Use of Morals.

Use of Comedyes.

Versibus exponi tragicis res comica non vult.

Againe Horace, *Arte Poeticá,*

At vestri proavi Plautinos et numeros et Laudavere sales.

If a comedy, it is pleasantly contrived with merry accidents, and intermixt with apt and witty jests, to present before the prince at certain times of solemnity, or else merily fitted to the stage.   And what is then the subject of this harmlesse mirth ? either in the shape of a clowne to shew others their slovenly and unhandsome behaviour, that they may reforme that simplicity in themselves which others make their sport, lest they happen to become the like subject of generall scorne to an auditory ; else it intreates of love, deriding foolish inamorates, who spend their ages, their spirits, nay themselves, in the servile and ridiculous imployments of their mistresses : and these are mingled with sportfull accidents, to recreate such as of themelves are wholly devoted to melancholly, which corrupts the bloud, or to refresh such weary spirits as are tired with labour or study, to moderate the cares and heavinesse of the minde, that they may returne to their trades and faculties with more zeale and earnestnesse, after some small, soft, and pleasant retirement. Sometimes they discourse of pantaloones, usurers that have unthrifty sonnes, which both the fathers and sonnes may behold to their instructions : sometimes of curtezans, to divulge their subtelties and snares in which young men may be intangled, shewing them the meanes to avoyd them.   If we present a pastorall, we shew the harmlesse love

Use of Pastorals.   of sheepheards diversely moralized, distinguishing betwixt the craft of the citty, and the innocency of the sheep-coat.   Briefly, there is neither tragedy, history, comedy, morrall, or pastorall, from which an infinite use cannot be gathered.   I speake not in the defence of any lascivious shewes, scurrelous jeasts, or scandalous invectives.   If there be any such I banish them quite from my patronage ; yet Horace, Sermon I., satyr iv., thus writes :—

Eupolis atque Cratinus Aristophanesque poetæ,
Atque alii quorum comœdia prisca virorum est,
Si quis erat dignus describi, quòd malus, aut fur,

Quòd mæchus foret, aut sicarius, aut alioqui
Famosus, multá cum libertate notabant.

Eupolis, Cratinus, Aristophanes, and other comike poets in the time of Horace, with large scope and unbridled liberty, boldly and plainly scourged all abuses, as in their ages were generally practised, to the staining and blemishing of a faire and beautifull common-weale. Likewise a learned gentleman in his Apology for Poetry speakes thus : Tragedies well handled be a most worthy kind of poesie. Comedies make men see and shame at their faults : and, proceeding further, amongst other University-playes he remembers the Tragedy of Richard the third, acted in St. Johns, in Cambridge, so essentially, that had the tyrant Phalaris beheld his bloudy proceedings, it had mollified his heart, and made him relent at sight of his inhuman massacres. Further, he commends of comedies, the Cambridge *Pedantius*, and the Oxford *Bellum Grammaticale;* and, leaving them, passes on to our publicke playes, speaking liberally in their praise, and what commendable use may be gathered of them. If you peruse *Margarita Poetica*, you may see what excellent uses and sentences he hath gathered out of *Terence* his *Andrea, Eunuchus,* and the rest : likewise out of *Plautus,* his *Amphytryo, Asinaria ;* and, moreover, *ex Comediis Philodoxis, Caroli Acretini: De falsá Hypocritá, et tristi Mercurio, Ronsii Versellensis : ex Comædiá Philanirá, Ugolini Parmensis,* all reverend schollers, and comicke poets. Reade elce the 4 tragedies, *Philunica, Petrus, Aman, Katherina, Claudii Roiletti Belvensis.* But I should tire my selfe to reckon the names of all French, Roman, German, Spanish, Italian, and English poets, being in number infinite, and their labours extant to approve their worthinesse.

Is thy minde noble, and wouldst thou be further stir'd up to magnanimity ? Behold upon the stage thou maist see Hercules, Achilles, Alexander, Cæsar, Alcibiades, Lysander,

Sertorius, Hannibal, Antigonus, Philip of Macedon, Mithridates of Pontus, Pyrrhus of Epirus: Agesilaus among the Lacedemonians; Epaminondas amongst the Thebans: Scævola alone entring the armed tents of Porsenna: Horatius Cocles alone withstanding the whole army of the Hetrurians: Leonidas of Sparta choosing a lyon to leade a band of deere, rather then one deere to conduct an army of lyons, with infinite others, in their own persones, qualities, and shapes, animating thee with courage, deterring thee from cowardise.   Hast thou of thy country well deserved? and art thou of thy labour evil requited?   To associate thee thou mayst see the valiant Roman Marcellus pursue Hannibal at Nola, conquering Syracusa, vanquishing the Gauls at Padua, and presently (for his reward) banisht his country into Greece.   There thou mayest see Scipio Africanus, now triumphing for the conquest of all Africa, and immediately exil'd the confines of Romania. Art thou inclined to lust? behold the falles of the Tarquins in the rape of Lucrece; the guerdon of luxury in the death of Sardanapalus; Appius destroyed in the ravishing of Virginia, and the destruction of Troy in the lust of Helena.   Art thou proud? our scene presents thee with the fall of Phaeton; Narcissus pining in the love of his shadow; ambitious Hamon, now calling himselfe a God, and by and by thrust headlong among the divels. We present men with the uglinesse of their vices to make them the more to abhorre them; as the Persians use, who, above all sinnes loathing drunkennesse, accustomed in their solemne feasts to make their servants and captives extremely overcome with wine, and then call their children to view their nasty and lothsome behaviour, making them hate that sinne in themselves, which shewed so grosse and abhominable in others.   The like use may be gathered of the drunkards, so naturally imitated in our playes, to the applause of the actor, content of the auditory, and reproving of the vice. Art thou covetous? go no further then Plautus, his comedy called Euclio.

Dum fallax servus, durus pater, improba lena
Vixerit, et meretrix blanda, Menandros erit.

While ther's false servant, or obdurate sire,
Sly baud, smooth whore, Menandros wee'l admire.

To end in a word, art thou addicted to prodigallity, envy, cruelty, perjury, flattery, or rage? our scenes affoord thee store of men to shape your lives by, who be frugall, loving, gentle, trusty, without soothing, and in all things temperate. Wouldst thou be honourable, just, friendly, moderate, devout, mercifull, and loving concord? thou mayest see many of their fates and ruines who have beene dishonourable, injust, false, gluttenous, sacrilegious, bloudy-minded, and brochers of dissention. Women, likewise, that are chaste are by us extolled and encouraged in their vertues, being instanced by Diana, Belphœbe, Matilda, Lucrece, and the Countess of Salisbury. The unchaste are by us shewed their errors in the persons of Phryne, Lais, Thais, Flora; and amongst us Rosamond and Mistresse Shore. What can sooner print modesty in the soules of the wanton, then by discovering unto them the monstrousnesse of their sin? It followes, that we prove these exercises to have beene the discoverers of many notorious murders, long concealed from the eyes of the world. To omit all farre-fetcht instances, we will prove it by a domestike and home-borne truth, which within these few years happened. At Lin, in Norfolke, the then Earl of Sussex players acting the old History of Feyer Francis, and presenting a woman who, insatiately doting on a *A strange accident happening at a play.* yong gentleman, (the more securely to enjoy his affection) mischievously and secreetly murdered her husband, whose ghost haunted her; and, at divers times, in her most solitary and private contemplations, in most horrid and feareful shapes, appeared and stood before her. As this was acted, a towne's-woman (till then of good estimation and report) finding her conscience (at this presentment) extremely troubled, suddenly

skritched and cryd out, Oh ! my husband, my husband ! I see
the ghost of my husband fiercely threatning and menacing me !
At which shrill and unexpected outcry, the people about her,
moov'd to a strange amazement, inquired the reason of her
clamour, when presently, un-urged, she told them that seven
yeares ago she, to be possest of such a gentleman (meaning
him), had poysoned her husband, whose fearefull image personated it selfe in the shape of that ghost. Whereupon the
murdresse was apprehended, before the justices further exa-
mined, and by her voluntary confession after condemned. That
this is true, as well by the report of the actors as the records
of the towne, there are many eyewitnesses of this accident yet
living vocally to confirme it.

<table>
<tr><td>A strange
accident hap-
pening at a
play.</td><td>As strange an accident happened to a company
of the same quality some 12 yeares ago, or not
so much ; who, playing late in the night, at a place</td></tr>
</table>

called Perin in Cornwall, certaine Spaniards were landed the
same night, unsuspected and undiscovered, with intent to take
in the towne, spoyle, and burne it, when suddenly, even upon
their entrance, the players (ignorant as the towne's-men of
any such attempt) presenting a battle on the stage, with their
drum and trumpets strooke up a lowde alarme : which the
enemy hearing, and fearing they were discovered, amazedly
retired, made some few idle shot, in a bravado, and so, in a
hurly-burly, fled disorderly to their boats. At the report of
this tumult, the towne's-men were immediately armed, and
pursued them to the sea, praysing God for their happy deliver-
ance from so great a danger, who by his providence made
these strangers the instrument and secondary meanes of their
escape from such imminent mischife, and the tyranny of so
remorceless an enemy.

<table>
<tr><td>A strange
accident
happening
at a play.</td><td>Another of the like wonder happened at Am-
sterdam in Holland. A company of our English
comedians (well knowne) travelling those coun-
tryes, as they were before the burgers and other</td></tr>
</table>

the chiefe inhabitants, acting the last part of the Four Sons of Aymon, towards the last act of the history, where penitent Rinaldo, like a common labourer, lived in disguise, vowing as his last pennance to labour and carry burdens to the structure of a goodly church there to be erected; whose diligence the labourers envying, since by reason of his stature and strength, hee did usually perfect more worke in a day then a dozen of the best (hee working for his conscience, they for their lucres), whereupon, by reason his industry had so much disparaged their living, conspired among themselves to kill him, waiting some opportunity to finde him asleepe, which they might easily doe, since the sorest labourers are the soundest sleepers, and industry is the best preparative to rest. Having spy'd their opportunity, they drave a naile into his temples, of which wound immediatly he dyed. As the actors handled this, the audience might on a sodaine understand an out-cry, and loud shrike in a remote gallery; and pressing about the place, they might perceive a woman of great gravity strangely amazed, who with a distracted and troubled braine oft sighed out these words: " Oh, my husband, my husband !" The play, without further interruption, proceeded: the woman was to her owne house conducted, without any apparant suspition; every one conjecturing as their fancies led them. In this agony she some few dayes languished, and on a time, as certaine of her well disposed neighbours came to comfort her, one amongst the rest being church-warden: to him the sexton posts, to tell him of a strange thing happening to him in the ripping up of a grave: See here (quoth he) what I have found; and shewes them a faire skull, with a great nayle pierst quite through the braine-pan: But we cannot conjecture to whom it should belong, nor how long it hath laine in the earth, the grave being confused, and the flesh consumed. At the report of this accident, the woman, out of the trouble of her afflicted conscience, discovered a former murder; for 12 yeares ago, by driving that nayle into that skull, being the head of her husband, she had trecherously slaine him. This being publickly confest, she was arraigned, condemned, adjudged, and burned. But I draw my subject to greater length then I purposed : these therefore out of other infinites I have collected, both for their familiarnesse and latenesse of memory.

Thus, our antiquity we have brought from the Grecians in the time of Hercules ; from the Macedonians in the age of Alexander ; from the Romans long before Julius Cæsar ; and since him, through the reigns of 23 emperours succeeding, even to Marcus Aurelius : after him they were supported by the Mantuans, Venetians, Valencians, Neapolitans, the Florentines, and others : since, by the German princes, the Palsgrave, the Landsgrave, the dukes of Saxony, of Brounswicke, &c. The cardinall at Bruxels hath at this time in pay a company of our English comedians. The French king allowes certaine companies in Paris, Orleans, besides other cities : so doth the king of Spaine, in Civill, Madrill, and other provinces. But in no country they are of that eminence that our's are : so our most royall and ever renouned soveraigne hath licenced us in London : so did his predecessor, the thrice vertuous virgin, Queene Elizabeth ; and before her, her sister, Queene Mary, Edward the sixth, and their father, Henry the eighth : and before these, in the tenth yeare of the reigne of Edward the fourth, *Anno* 1490. John Stowe, an ancient and grave chronicler, records (amongst other varieties tending to the like effect) that a play was acted at a place called Skinners-well, fast by Clerken-well, which continued eight dayes, and was of matter from Adam and Eve (the first creation of the world). The spectators were no worse then the royalty of England. And amongst other commendable exercises in this place, the Company of the Skinners of London held certaine yearely solemne playes ; in place whereof, now in these latter daies, the wrastling, and such other pastimes have been kept, and is still held about Bartholmewtide. Also in the yeare 1390, the 14 yeare of the reigne of

Richard the second, the 18 of July, were the like enterludes recorded of at the same place, which continued 3 dayes together, the king and queene, and nobility being there present. Moreover, to this day in divers places of England there be townes that hold the priviledge of their faires, and other charters by yearely stage-playes, as at Manningtree in Suffolke, Kendall in the north, and others. To let these passe, as things familiarly knowne to all men. Now, to speake of some abuse lately crept into the quality, as an inveighing against the state, the court, the law, the citty, and their governements, with the particularizing of private men's humors (yet alive), noble-men, and others : I know it distastes many ; neither do I any way approve it, nor dare I by any meanes excuse it. The liberty which some arrogate to themselves, committing their bitternesse, and liberall invectives against all estates, to the mouthes of children, supposing their juniority to be a priviledge for any rayling, be it never so violent, I could advise all such to curbe and limit this presumed liberty within the bands of discretion and government. But wise and judiciall censurers, before whom such complaints shall at any time hereafter come, wil not (I hope) impute these abuses to any transgression in us, who have ever been carefull and provident to shun the like. I surcease to prosecute this any further, lest my good meaning be (by some) misconstrued ;

and fearing likewise, lest with tediousnesse I tire the

patience of the favourable Reader, heere

(though abruptly) I conclude

my third and last

TREATISE.

Stultitiam patiuntur opes, mihi parvula res est.

To my approved good Friend,

MR. NICHOLAS OKES.

THE infinite faults escaped in my booke of Britaines Troy
by the negligence of the printer, as the misquotations, mis-
taking of sillables, misplacing halfe lines, coining of strange
and never heard of words, these being without number,
when I would have taken a particular account of the *errata*,
the printer answered me, hee would not publish his owne dis-
workemanship, but rather let his owne fault lye upon the
necke of the author. And being fearefull that others of his
quality had beene of the same nature and condition, and finding you, on the contrary, so carefull and industrious, so serious
and laborious to doe the author all the rights of the presse, I
could not choose but gratulate your honest indeavours with
this short remembrance. Here, likewise, I must necessarily
insert a manifest injury done me in that worke, by taking the
two epistles of Paris to Helen, and Helen to Paris, and
printing them in a lesse volume under the name of another,
which may put the world in opinion I might steale them from
him, and hee, to doe himselfe right, hath since published them
in his owne name : but, as I must acknowledge my lines not
worthy his patronage under whom he hath publisht them, so
the author, I know, much offended with M. Jaggard (that altogether unknowne to him), presumed to make so bold with
his name. These and the like dishonesties I knowe
you to bee cleere of ; and I could wish but to
bee the happy author of so worthy a
worke as I could willingly commit to your care and
workmanship.

Yours, ever,
THOMAS HEYWOOD.

NOTES.

Page 4, line 9. I need alledge no more then the royall and princely services in which we now live.] Alluding to the fact that, on the accession of James I., the king took into his service the Lord Chamberlain's players, the queen those of the Earl of Worcester, and Prince Henry those of the Earl of Nottingham. *Vide* " Memoirs of Edward Alleyn," p. 61, *Note.*

Page 4, line 22. Learned Doctor Gager, Doctor Gentiles, and others.] Drs. Gager and Gentiles were the adversaries of Dr. Rainoldes in the " controversy" which ended in the publication of " The Overthrow of Stage Playes," by the latter, in 1599 or 1600.

Page 4, line 31. True gatherers.] The " gatherers" were what we now call the money-takers at the doors of theatres. Actors at this time were generally " sharers" of the profits, and faithful receivers of money paid on admission were therefore important. See the term more fully explained in " Hist. Engl. Dram. Poetry and the Stage," III. 403.

Page 8, line 21. Ar. Hopton.] The author of these laudatory stanzas died two years after they were printed. He was a young man of extraordinary attainments and promise. *Vide* Wood's *Ath. Oxon,* II. 151. Edit. Bliss.

Page 9, line 20. John Webster.] All that was then known about this highly-gifted dramatic author was collected and published by the Rev. A. Dyce, in his edition of Webster's Works, 4 vols. post 8vo., 1830. Henslowe's Diary supplies information of much interest respecting some lost productions by Webster.

Page 10, line 27. Rich. Perkins.] The name of this actor, who did not attain his highest eminence until some years after 1612, occurs in Henslowe's Diary. For him Marlowe's " Rich Jew of Malta " was revived by Heywood, and printed in 1633.

Page 11, line 13. Christopher Beeston.] This actor's name also occurs late in Henslowe's Diary. He afterwards became a player at the Cockpit theatre in Drury Lane, for which Heywood wrote ; and in 1636 he was the master of a company of juvenile performers.

Page 11, line 22.   Robert Pallant.]   This actor subsequently joined the King's Company, and arrived at some eminence.

Page 12, line 34.   John Taylor.]   This person is not to be confounded with Joseph Taylor, the actor, who has been mistakenly supposed to have been the original Hamlet, a part which was first sustained by Richard Burbage.   John Taylor was known as " the Water-poet," because he commenced life as apprentice to a waterman, and for some years followed the occupation.   He was an extremely voluminous author, and his collected works were printed in 1630, folio.

Page 15, line 18.   It hath pleased the high and mighty Princes of this land to limit the use of certain publicke theaters.]   This passage appears to refer to the orders of the Privy Council to limit the number of theatres in use at the end of the reign of Elizabeth.   *Vide* " Hist. of Engl. Dram. Poetry and the Stage," I. 311, &c.

Page 15, line 26.   To stop the envious acclamations of those who chalenge to themselves a priveledge invective, &c.]   This passage, and some others of the same kind, refer generally to such works as the " Invective " of Stephen Gosson, under the title of " the School of Abuse," " the Anatomy of Abuses," by Philip Stubbes, &c.

Page 16, line 27.   I might behold the colour of her fresh roabe, all crimson breathed, &c.]   This expression is further explained by a line in the blank-verse speech, which Heywood subsequently puts into the mouth of Melpomene:

" Such with their breath have blasted my fresh roabe."

Page 23, line 11.   If such rich wages thou wilt give to me.]   These concluding lines had already been used by Gosson in his " School of Abuse." *Vide* p. 19 of our reprint.

Page 29, line 15.   It instructs him to fit his phrases to his action, and his action to his phrase.]   So Hamlet, Act III., Scene 2—" Suit the action to the word, the word to the action."

Page 40, line 10.   The king of Denmarke, father to him that now reigneth, entertained into his service a company of English comedians.] See also p. 58, where it is said that an English company was performing in Amsterdam.   No date is given, but circumstances shew that it must have been subsequent to 1602.

Page 43, line 6.   Knell, Bentley, Mils, Wilson, Crosse, Lanam, and others, these, since I never saw them, as being before my time, &c.]   We may conclude from this passage that these celebrated actors were dead before 1596, which, as has been shown in the Introduction, was, in all probability, the date of Heywood's earliest connection with the stage.

Page 43, line 13. *Here I must needs remember Tarleton, in his time gratious with the queene.*] Richard Tarlton died in September, 1588. Many materials for a separate life of this extraordinary actor might be collected: he has furnished some of them himself, and he is mentioned by many writers of his own time and afterwards.

Page 43, line 16. *Whom succeeded Wil. Kemp.*] Thomas Nash, about 1589, the year after Tarlton's death, calls Kemp " Jest-monger and Vicegerent general to the Ghost of Dicke Tarlton." There are several entries in Henslowe's Diary, shewing that Kemp belonged to the company acting under Alleyn's management in 1602, although he had been one of the Lord Chamberlain's players, in 1596. He probably commenced as an actor with Alleyn about 1586 or 1587, then joined the association to which Shakespeare was attached, and finally returned to his old quarters.

Page 43, line 18. *Gabriel.*] i. e., Gabriel Spencer, who was killed by Ben Jonson—*Vide* " Memoirs of Edward Alleyn," page 51. He seems to have been generally known by his christian name; and so he is spoken of by Henslowe, in his letter of 26th September, 1598. This opportunity may be taken to correct an error in the " Memoirs of Edward Alleyn," where it is said that two persons of the christian name of Gabriel belonged to Henslowe's company in 1598; viz., Gabriel Spencer and Gabriel Singer. The name of the latter was John Singer, and no Gabriel Singer occurs in Henslowe's Diary. The mistake originated, probably, in Collier's " Hist. of Engl. Dram. Poetry and the Stage," I. 351., where " Gabriel" is misprinted for *John*.

Page 43, line 26. *They should be rather schollers.*] We ought, perhaps, to read *either* for " rather."

Page 44, line 26. *A booke called Wit's Commonwealth.*] The celebrated work, by Francis Meres, printed in 1598, 12mo., which contains, on Sig. O o 2, the often-quoted enumeration of twelve of Shakespeare's dramas, including " Love's Labours Won," and " Titus Andronicus."

Page 45, line 24. *Therefore M. Kid, in his Spanish Tragedy, upon occasion presenting itselfe, thus writes.*] The lines here quoted by Heywood occur in Act V. of the " Spanish Tragedy." It is upon Heywood's authority that the play has been attributed to Thomas Kyd.

Page 49, line 20. *ἀχιν δονος πορoιχην.*] So it stands in the original; and it is, perhaps, impossible now to set the corruption right, as Heywood does not quote his authority.

Page 55, line 7. *Likewise a learned gentleman in his Apology for Poetry.*] Heywood here quotes from Sir John Harington's " Apologie of Poetrie," prefixed to his translation of Ariosto's *Orlando Furioso* in 1591.

F

Page 58, line 6. Meaning him.] " Meaning" is misprinted in the original for *naming*. Cartwright did not detect and correct the error in his re-
impression. In the same way, in line 17, he allowed " Perin, in Cornwall,"
to stand, instead of *Penrin,* or *Penryn.*

Page 61, line 8. Now to speake of some abuse lately crept into the
quality, as inveighing against the state, &c.] The following passage from
the epistle before H. Parrot's " More the Merrier," 4to., 1608, will not be
out of place :—" As for satyrick inveighing at any man's private person (a
kind of writing which, of late, seemes to have been very familiar among our
poets and players, to their cost), my reader is to seeke it elsewhere." See
also, upon this point, a very curious account in Von Raumer's " History of
the Sixteenth and Seventeenth Centuries," (II. 219) of the interference of
the French Ambassador in April, 1606, to punish the actors and put a stop
to the performance of Chapman's play, on the Life of the Duke of Biron,
in consequence of the introduction of the Queen of France into it, giving a
box on the ear to Mademoiselle de Verneuil. From the same work it
appears that James I. had been represented on the stage two days before.

Page 62, line 15. Here, likewise, I must necessarily insert a manifest
injury done to me, &c.] This passage establishes that the edition of " The
Passionate Pilgrim," with the date of 1612, was published before Heywood's
" Apology for Actors" came out in the same year. It was in that work
that Jaggard, the careless and fraudulent printer, inserted " the two
Epistles of Paris to Helen, and Helen to Paris," which Heywood had
translated in his " Great Britain's Troy." Jaggard attributed them to
Shakespeare. .Malone had a copy of " The Passionate Pilgrim," with two
title-pages; in one of which a correction was made, perhaps, in consequence
of Heywood's remonstrance.

FINIS.

LONDON:

F. SHOBERL, JUN., 51, RUPERT STREET, HAYMARKET,

PRINTER TO H. R. H. PRINCE ALBERT.

Printed in Great Britain
by Amazon.co.uk, Ltd.,
Marston Gate.